D0978954

Issues in
Racism

Other books in the Contemporary Issues series:

CONTEMPORARY ISSUES

Issues in Racism

by Mary E. Williams

Lucent Books, San Diego, CA

Library of Congress Cataloging-in-Publication Data

Williams, Mary E., 1960–
  Issues in racism / by Mary E. Williams
    p. cm.—(Contemporary issues)
Includes bibliographical references and index.
Summary: Discusses various issues regarding racism, including racial profiling, police brutality, stereotyping, white privilege, and the need for dialogue.
  ISBN 1-56006-478-1 (alk. paper)
  1. United States—Race relations—Juvenile literature. 2. Racism—United States—Juvenile literature. 3. Race discrimination—United States—4. Affirmative action programs—United States—Juvenile literature. [1. Race relations. 2. Racism. 3. Race discrimination. 4. Discrimination.] I. Title. II. Contemporary issues (San Diego, Calif.)
  E184.A1 W46   2000
  305.8'00973—dc21   00-008052

TABLE OF CONTENTS

Foreword

When men are brought face to face with their opponents, forced to listen and learn and mend their ideas, they cease to be children and savages and begin to live like civilized men. Then only is freedom a reality, when men may voice their opinions because they must examine their opinions.

Walter Lippmann, American editor and writer

CONTROVERSY FOSTERS DEBATE. The very mention of a controversial issue prompts listeners to choose sides and offer opinion. But seeing beyond one's opinions is often difficult. As Walter Lippmann implies, true reasoning comes from the ability to appreciate and understand a multiplicity of viewpoints. This ability to assess the range of opinions is not innate; it is learned by the careful study of an issue. Those who wish to reason well, as Lippmann attests, must be willing to examine their own opinions even as they weigh the positive and negative qualities of the opinions of others.

The *Contemporary Issues* series explores controversial topics through the lens of opinion. The series addresses some of today's most debated issues and, drawing on the diversity of opinions, presents a narrative that reflects the controversy surrounding those issues. All of the quoted testimonies are taken from primary sources and represent both prominent and lesser-known persons who have argued these topics. For example, the title on biomedical ethics contains the views of physicians commenting on both sides of the physician-assisted suicide issue: Some wage a moral argument that assisted suicide allows patients to die with dignity, while others assert that assisted suicide violates the Hippocratic oath. Yet the book also includes the opinions of those who see the issue in a more personal way. The relative of a person who died by assisted suicide feels the loss of a loved one and makes a plaintive cry against it, while companions of another assisted suicide victim attest that their friend no longer wanted to endure the agony of a slow death. The profusion of quotes illustrates the range of thoughts and emotions that impinge on any debate. Displaying the range of perspectives, the series is designed to show how personal belief—whether informed by statistical evidence, religious conviction, or public opinion—shapes and complicates arguments.

Each title in the *Contemporary Issues* series discusses multiple controversies within a single field of debate. The title on environmental issues, for example, contains one chapter that asks whether the Endangered Species Act should be repealed, while another asks if Americans can afford the economic and social costs of environmentalism. Narrowing the focus of debate to a specific question, each chapter sharpens the competing perspectives and investigates the philosophies and personal convictions that inform these viewpoints.

Students researching contemporary issues will find this format particularly useful in uncovering the central controversies of topics by placing them in a moral, economic, or political context that allows the students to easily see the points of disagreement. Because of this structure, the series provides an excellent launching point for further research. By clearly defining major points of contention, the series also aids readers in critically examining the structure and source of debates. While providing a resource on which to model persuasive essays, the quoted opinions also permit students to investigate the credibility and usefulness of the evidence presented.

For students contending with current issues, the ability to assess the credibility, usefulness, and persuasiveness of the testimony as well as the factual evidence given by the quoted experts is critical not only in judging the merits of these arguments but in analyzing the students' own beliefs. By plumbing the logic of another person's opinions, readers will be better able to assess their own thinking. And this, in turn, can promote the type of introspection that leads to a conviction based on reason. Though *Contemporary Issues* offers the opportunity to shape one's own opinions in light of competing or concordant philosophies, above all, it shows readers that well-reasoned, well-intentioned arguments can be countered by opposing opinions of equal worth.

Critically examining one's own opinions as well as the opinions of others is what Walter Lippmann believes makes an individual "civilized." Developing the skill early can only aid a reader's understanding of both moral conviction and political action. For students, a facility for reasoning is indispensable. Comprehending the foundations of opinions leads the student to the heart of controversy— to a recognition of what is at stake when holding a certain viewpoint. But the goal is not detached analysis; the issues are often far too immediate for that. The *Contemporary Issues* series induces the reader not only to see the shape of a current controversy, but to engage it, to respond to it, and ultimately to find one's place within it.

Introduction ◼

Defining Racism

O N A JUNE EVENING IN 1998, a disabled middle-aged black man
named James Byrd Jr. was hitchhiking home after attending his
niece's bridal shower near Jasper, Texas. When three young white
men in a pickup truck stopped to offer him a ride, Byrd climbed in
and accompanied the men to a market where they refueled their
vehicle. As they got back on the road, however, the truck headed
eastward out of town. The driver stopped in a remote wooded area,
and the men pulled Byrd out of the truck. They kicked him until he
was unable to move and chained his ankles to the truck's back
bumper. Then they dragged Byrd for two miles down the rough road
until his body was beheaded and torn into pieces.

James Byrd Jr. was tortured and killed solely because he was
black, and Americans were shocked by the grisliness of the crime.
This murder brought back frightening memories of the racially segregated South prior to the civil rights movement of the 1950s and
1960s. During that time, African Americans were frequently terror-
ized by racist whites intent on subjugating blacks and keeping the
races separate. By the late 1990s, however, such horrifying demon-
strations of racism were considered indefensible and immoral by
society at large.

Progress in Race Relations

In some ways the outpouring of sympathy and concern following
Byrd's murder reveals how much race relations have improved since
the middle of the twentieth century. Comparing Byrd's case with the
Emmett Till murder case of the mid-1950s reveals this progress. Till
was a fourteen-year-old black boy who was lynched by white men in

Ross Byrd, son of James Byrd Jr., wipes a tear from his sister's face after John William King, one of James Byrd's killers, was found guilty.

Mississippi in 1955. Despite strong proof pointing to Till's killers, their court trial resulted in a "not guilty" verdict from an all-white jury. In his response to the verdict, civil rights activist Roy Wilkins declared that "the killer of the boy felt free to lynch because there is in the entire state [of Mississippi] no restraining influence of decency, not in the state capital, among the daily newspapers, the clergy, not among any segment of the so-called lettered citizens."[1]

In Texas in 1998, however, the town of Jasper grieved in the wake of Byrd's murder, with black and white ministers leading eight thousand citizens in prayer vigils and interracial rallies. Investigators acted swiftly to arrest and indict the three men suspected of murdering Byrd. They were all found guilty by a predominantly white jury, and two of the killers received death sentences.

Jasper's local leaders immediately condemned the poisonous racism that had led to Byrd's murder: "This is not Jasper," they declared. President Bill Clinton agreed, insisting that "this is not what this country is all about."[2] Such public outcry against bigotry suggests, to many observers, that the United States as a nation is no longer constrained by the racism that so often defined its past.

Continuing Racial Injustice

Not everyone agrees that America has largely overcome racism. In his commentary on the events in Jasper, news columnist Carl Rowan argues that the murder of Byrd "reflects the hatred of more people in this country than most Americans want to admit." In truth, violent murders resulting from racial hatred are relatively rare today. However, such bias-motivated crimes are simply the most extreme form of a more widespread problem, contends Rowan:

> The murder of James Byrd Jr. was so gruesome that most Americans have no trouble deploring it and trying to disassociate [distance] themselves from it. What we all need to understand is that every day thousands of human beings are deeply wounded by acts of racism—in personnel offices, apartment rental agencies, police departments and corporate boardrooms. . . . Only when we truly stand up against the day-to-day racial injustices can we say honestly of a grotesque murder, "This is not my town. This is not America."[3]

Defining Racism

To understand what Rowan means by the phrase *acts of racism*, it is important to recognize that the word *racism* is used in different ways. In everyday speech people may use the word *racism* to refer to the belief that one race is superior to another or to one person's hatred of another because of differences in skin color and other physical traits. However, in public debates about American racism, social analysts often define racism in a broader context.

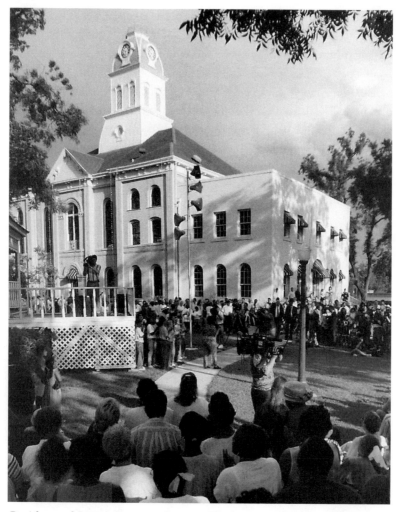

Residents of Jasper, Texas, gather outside the Jasper County Courthouse
for a prayer vigil on June 15, 1998, in memory of James Byrd Jr.

These analysts stress historical truths about race relations in the
United States. Many point out, for example, that whites have long
comprised the majority of those who control U.S. politics and culture. Because of their majority status, whites as a group have the
power to assert racial prejudice and deny minorities opportunities to
succeed in society. This situation has created, in author David Well-
man's words, "a system of advantage based on race."[4]

In her discussion of racism as a system of unfair privilege, educator Beverly Daniel Tatum notes that "racism . . . is not only a personal ideology based on racial prejudices, but a *system* involving cultural messages and institutional policies and practices. . . . In the context of the United States, this system clearly operates to the advantage of whites and to the disadvantage of people of color."[5]

This definition of *racism*, however, should not be taken to mean that all whites subscribe to racism. Nor does it mean that minorities are incapable of harboring racial prejudices that, if acted on, can hurt whites or other people of color. Describing racism as a system of advantage does not accuse all whites of bigotry or deny the potential for racial hatred among people of color. Rather, this definition emphasizes racism as a social force that affects people of color differently than it affects whites.

Racial Discrimination Today

Today's racism, as Rowan, Tatum, and others argue, rarely takes the form of racially motivated hate crimes. But troubling incidents involving racism do occur. Throughout the 1990s, for example, lawsuits against Denny's, Shoney's, and the International House of Pancakes (IHOP) were filed by minority customers claiming that they were discriminated against. In one of these cases, several groups of black college students had been turned away from a Milwaukee IHOP— restaurant workers told them that the restaurant was closed, but white customers were allowed in. In recent years, moreover, numerous black and Latino motorists have charged that they have been pulled over by police officers, questioned, and searched even though they had committed no traffic violations. Some people contend that police officers often stereotype minorities as prone to violent and criminal behavior. Such a stereotype can encourage the police to aggressively pursue—and on occasion even brutalize— people of color.

Perhaps most prevalent, many commentators argue, are the hidden forms of racism that can thwart life opportunities for minorities. This kind of racism includes the subtle discrimination that occurs in workplaces, schools, and other societal institutions. Examples of this discrimination can be seen in some recently publicized studies

California demonstrators voice their support for affirmative action, a program designed to increase educational and economic opportunities for minorities.

on race relations. Throughout the 1990s, several organizations and news groups conducted research in which whites, blacks, and Latinos were sent out to apply for jobs, fill out rental applications, and buy cars. All of the participants were dressed similarly and were given the same information to write down on application forms. The sole difference among the research participants was their race. Again and again, researchers discovered, the white participants were offered jobs, apartments, and good prices on cars. The minorities, however, were frequently denied work and housing and were charged higher prices for cars. Although the black and Latino research participants were generally treated politely by employers, apartment managers, and car dealers, the white participants were given opportunities that were often denied to those of color.

These studies, many point out, reveal the racism that can lie behind polite behavior. Whites in positions of power who harbor racist assumptions, such as the stereotype that African Americans are lazy, may treat blacks equitably in social situations—yet also deny them the chance for a job or a promotion. Some social analysts maintain that "racial tensions cannot be resolved until white Americans admit to these racist assumptions and openly acknowledge the current prevalence of racism."[6]

Does Racism Hold Minorities Back?

Many people, on the other hand, contend that racism is no longer a serious problem in the United States. While they may agree that racism still exists, they do not believe it currently has the power to keep minorities from pursuing and accomplishing their dreams. Some commentators point to the large numbers of African Americans who have achieved social, educational, and financial success in recent decades as proof that racism no longer holds minorities back. Scholars Abigail and Stephan Thernstrom point out, for example, that while 87 percent of blacks lived in poverty in 1940, 75 percent of black married couples today consider themselves middle-class. Hispanics also have grown increasingly successful, claims commentator Linda Chavez: "[Hispanics] work hard, support their own families without outside assistance, [and] have more education and higher earnings than their parents."[7] Even if hidden discrimination still occurs, these analysts argue, it cannot change the positive direction of minority progress.

Some also maintain that today's whites are unfairly accused of racism. According to the Thernstroms, whites' attitudes about blacks have actually undergone a vast transformation in the last half of the twentieth century. They point out that in 1942, half of all northern whites believed blacks were significantly less intelligent than whites; by 1956, only 17 percent of northern whites believed that blacks were less intelligent. In 1966, during the civil rights movement, 71 percent of whites said they would not object to blacks with the same education and income moving into their neighborhood.

Furthermore, several recent surveys suggest that a majority of whites believe that racial discrimination is practically nonexistent in America. One 1997 Gallup poll pointed out that most whites feel that there are plentiful opportunities for blacks and that incidents of racial prejudice are rare.

The Racial Divide

Much of the current debate about racism occurs between those who believe that racism is still a serious problem and those who do not. This split in public opinion tends to occur along racial lines, as can be seen in the results of a 1995 Roper survey that asked thousands of adults, "How big a problem is racism in our society today?" Sixty-seven percent of blacks claimed that racism was a big problem; 38 percent of whites drew the same conclusion. Forty-six percent of Hispanics believed racism was a big problem, and 50 percent of Asians claimed that racism was "somewhat of a problem."[8]

What accounts for such differences of opinion among Americans? Many people maintain that different life experiences often lead whites and minorities to draw opposite conclusions about the persistence of racism. For one thing, whites generally do not face the kinds of racial prejudice routinely encountered by people of color. Moreover, numerous whites go through life with no significant or long-term contact with people of other races. Because they

During World War II, Japanese Americans were sent to internment camps, including this one in Puyallup, Washington, because they were viewed as a threat to security.

do not experience much prejudice in their own lives or know many people who have experienced racial discrimination, whites may conclude that racism is not much of a problem today. On the other hand, minorities' frequent encounters with racial discrimination makes it more difficult for them to believe that the nation is serious about equal rights for all. Repeated experiences with racism can cause people of color to feel anger and cynicism about the future of race relations in the United States.

Certainly, despair about the future of race relations cannot lead to continuing progress. At the same time, progress is stalled when people are unable or unwilling to admit to racism's current realities. A successful battle against racism will require the energies of both whites and minorities. It behooves concerned people of all races to carefully examine why Americans continue to have such striking differences of opinion about the nature of racial stereotypes, prejudice, and discrimination. Education, honesty, and respectful communication between whites and people of color will be powerful allies in this ongoing struggle for racial understanding.

Chapter 1

How Serious a Problem Is Racism?

IT USUALLY TAKES FORTY MINUTES for Elmo Randolph, an African American dentist, to drive from his home to his office near Newark, New Jersey. But on many occasions he has been late to work—not because he overslept or faced unusually heavy traffic—because he was pulled over by New Jersey state troopers. In fact, between 1991 and 1999, Randolph was stopped by police on the New Jersey Turnpike more than fifty times. He was never given a speeding ticket or cited for erratic driving. Instead, Randolph reports, an officer would approach his gold BMW, request his driver's license and registration, and ask if he had any drugs or weapons in his car. Randolph contends that the only reason he has been stopped so often is because police are suspicious when they see a black man driving an expensive car: "Would they pull over a white middle-class person and ask the same question?"[9]

Black and Latino motorists often claim that they have been stopped and searched by law enforcement officers for no apparent reason other than the color of their skin. Furthermore, many argue, racial minorities are stopped by police far more often than white people are—especially if they are driving pricey cars or traveling through white neighborhoods. Because these traffic stops do not usually result in a ticket and appear to be racially motivated, they have been tagged with the sarcastic acronym "DWB"—Driving While Black (or Brown).

Statistics lend support to these charges. According to the New Jersey attorney general, 77 percent of the drivers stopped and searched by New Jersey state police are black or Hispanic, but only 13.5 percent of

18

motorists on New Jersey highways are black or Hispanic. In addition, one mid-1990s study conducted by the American Civil Liberties Union (ACLU) found that African Americans comprised 72 percent of the drivers pulled over on a Maryland interstate even though they represented only 14 percent of all drivers on that freeway.

Racial Profiling

Critics of law enforcement maintain that these statistics are the result of racial profiling—the use of race as a factor in identifying criminal suspects. Some social observers allege that police officers, most of whom are white, tend to see dark skin color as a sign of a person's potential criminality. The belief that minorities are prone to lawless behavior, many argue, causes police to disproportionately stop and search people of color.

In the late 1990s, public concern over the issue of racial profiling drew the attention of the federal government. President Bill Clinton ordered federal law enforcement agencies to gather information about their own police procedures to help determine the scope of the problem. At a 1999 Justice Department conference, the

Representative John Conyers introduces an act to gather information on police using racial profiling as a basis for traffic stops.

representatives of several national police organizations agreed with Clinton that the possibility of widespread racial bias in law enforcement needed to be addressed. Biased police actions, they feared, could lead people to believe that the law is not equally enforced and undermine the effectiveness and the authority of the police.

Not everyone agrees, however, that racial profiling presents a problem for the field of law enforcement. Some argue that police officers target minorities because they have a higher incidence of criminal activity. For instance, *U.S. News & World Report* states that blacks compose only 13 percent of the U.S. population but make up 35 percent of all drug arrests and 55 percent of all drug convictions. While critics allege that this large percentage of minority drug arrests is a result of police bias, some evidence suggests that minorities as a group use drugs at higher rates than whites do. The Department of Health and Human Services, which keeps statistics on people admitted to emergency rooms because of drug overdoses, reports that African Americans are admitted at seven times the white rate for heroin and morphine and ten times the white rate for cocaine. Moreover, Hispanics are admitted at two to three times the white rate for drug overdoses. Some observers contend that if relatively high percentages of minorities engage in illegal drug abuse and other crimes, police should not be accused of undue bias when they pursue people of color as possible criminal suspects.

Some people grant that there may be isolated incidents of racial bias among police. However, they argue that the claim of widespread racial profiling is largely a myth. As proof, they point to the fact that Asian Americans are stopped and arrested at consistently lower rates than are whites. As one commentator put it, "Wouldn't 'racist' cops think of some way to snare Asians?"[10]

Critics, however, disagree that the lower arrest rate for Asians indicates a lack of prejudice among police. It may simply prove that many police officers buy in to the common stereotype of Asians as unassertive and nonviolent. This may be a "positive" stereotype, but it is still a racial generalization that can lead to discriminatory and unequal applications of the law.

Furthermore, many critics dispute the claim that blacks and Latinos commit a disproportionate number of crimes and thereby justify law enforcement's targeting of minorities. They contend that accusations of racial profiling, when closely examined, usually do reveal a pattern of bias. One investigation, for example, looked at complaints received from black women who claimed that airport customs agents had strip-searched them for no reason. During one year at Chicago's O'Hare Airport, nearly half of the people who had been strip-searched for drugs were black women. When investigators delved further, they discovered that 90 percent of the black women who had been searched were not carrying any drugs. In fact, investigators found, black women were part of the group least likely to be carrying drugs, although they were eight times more likely to be searched than white males.

Being stopped and searched by law enforcement officials may not typically result in traffic tickets or arrests for people of color. However, many insist that such constant scrutiny by police is humiliating and emotionally draining. In addition, the possibility that police engage in racial profiling increases minorities' fears about being subjected to police brutality.

Differences of Opinion

Police bias and police brutality are issues that clearly reveal the difference of opinion that whites and minorities have about the seriousness of the problem of racism. In his discussion of an NBC poll of blacks and whites across the nation, news commentator Clarence Page reports that,

> when it comes to perceptions of the police, the poll shows the races to be living on different planets. For example, when asked, "How often does police brutality occur in your community?" 46 percent of whites said "almost never," compared to only 21 percent of blacks. Conversely, 41 percent of blacks agreed that "police treat blacks less fairly," compared to a measly 18 percent of whites.[11]

Why do many blacks and whites have such varying perceptions of the police? Differences in life experiences probably account for these conflicting opinions. On the one hand, the most frequent interaction that whites have with police officers involves minor traffic violations.

Drawing from their personal experiences, whites often conclude that police officers objectively enforce the law. Blacks, on the other hand, may recall being stopped, searched, and sometimes even harassed by the police even though they had committed no crimes. African Americans are more likely to conclude, therefore, that such incidents are typical of the treatment minorities receive from the police.

Throughout the 1990s, several allegations of physical abuse of minorities by police officers made national headlines. Many have vivid memories of the 1991 videotaped beating of black motorist Rodney King by white police officers in Los Angeles. An all-white jury acquitted four of these officers of brutality charges in 1992, sparking several days of rioting in which more than fifty people were killed. More recently, in 1997, police officers mistook Haitian immigrant Abner Louima for another black man who had punched a white officer at a New York City nightclub. Several police officers severely beat Louima and shoved the handle of a toilet plunger up his rectum, puncturing his bladder and intestines. Many social analysts contend that if King and Louima had been white, they would not have received such grossly abusive treatment from the police.

In response to such arguments, supporters of law enforcement assert that the news media exaggerate the problem of racist police brutality, overemphasizing the relevance of isolated incidents such as the ones involving King and Louima. The vast majority of police officers, they maintain, are well-intentioned professionals who do not act with abusive intolerance. Many civil rights groups, on the other hand, contend that police mistreatment of minorities indicates a more extensive problem of racial discrimination in law enforcement.

This dispute about the prevalence and seriousness of racial bias in law enforcement illustrates just one facet of today's controversy about racism in America. Politicians, business leaders, religious leaders, educators, activists, and the general public have an ongoing debate about whether racially prejudiced attitudes continue to permeate society. While many contend that racism still restricts freedoms and opportunities for minorities, others maintain that American society has largely overcome racism. Furthermore, whites and minorities often draw different conclusions about the nature of racial discrimination in the United States.

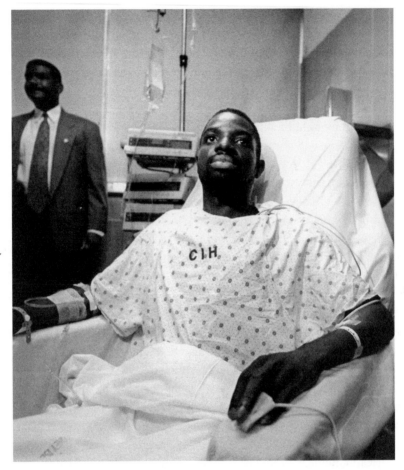

Abner Louima lies in the hospital in critical and guarded condition after his brutal attack by New York City police officers.

How Racial Stereotypes Develop

The broader debate about racism in America often focuses on the power that stereotypes have to negatively affect human relations. Stereotypes—simplistic and oftentimes disparaging opinions about groups—are typically the result of long-standing conflicts between certain groups. Racial stereotypes are usually scornful because they are opinions based on mutual group antagonism rather than friendly interaction.

Moreover, if one racial group claims power over another, members of the dominant group may use their negative beliefs about the other group to justify their own dominance. Europeans participating in the slave trade in the 1600s, for example, relied on their scornful opinions about Africans—particularly the notion that Africans were violent, uncivilized, and mentally inferior—to justify slavery. Historians point out that many Europeans and Americans believed that slavery was moral because it took blacks out of a "savage" environment and brought them into a "civilized" world.

Stereotypes and Racial Segregation

Many social analysts maintain that the history of black/white relations in the United States reveals the "staying power" of racial stereotypes. The belief that blacks were inferior to whites, for example, lingered long after the end of slavery. During the late 1800s and early 1900s, many whites, particularly southerners, supported social customs and laws that required the separation of the races in almost all aspects of life. Intended to ensure that blacks maintained a menial status in the absence of slavery, legalized segregation was also meant to "protect" whites from the distasteful attributes they had come to associate with blacks: violence, uncleanliness, and immorality.

As a result of such segregation, most African Americans did not have the same access that whites had to high-quality education and lucrative work. A large percentage of blacks lived in poverty, struggling to survive on subsistence wages. And for many whites living in the first half of the twentieth century, the fact that a majority of African Americans remained poor and uneducated only reinforced the stereotype of blacks as innately inferior.

In the 1950s public sentiment concerning race relations began to change, and a social movement involving civil rights organizations, labor unions, churches, and student groups started battling against the system of racial segregation. Subsequently, the government outlawed forced segregation and passed laws that made racial discrimination in housing and in employment illegal. White attitudes toward African Americans shifted, becoming less negative and more accepting. One study reveals that "in 1933, 75% of white respondents described blacks as lazy; in 1993, that figure declined to just 5%."[12] Moreover, 90 percent of whites polled in 1994 maintained that they would vote for a well-qualified black presidential

James Meredith, the first black student at the University of Mississippi. School integration was an important victory for the civil rights movement.

candidate; in 1958, almost no whites would claim support for a black candidate.

But much evidence suggests that many whites continue to hold disparaging views of blacks. In a national survey conducted in the 1990s by the Anti-Defamation League (ADL), white respondents were given a list of eight stereotypes of African Americans, including "more prone to violence," "less ambitious," and "less native intelligence." The ADL reports that "fully *76 percent* of this national random sample agreed with one or more of the antiblack stereotypes; 55 percent agreed with two or more stereotypes and about 30 percent agreed with four or more." While a majority of today's whites may hold fewer stereotypical attitudes than whites in the past, "slavery-era arguments are very much alive,"[13] maintains the ADL.

The Persistence of Racial Stereotypes

Many social analysts point out that stereotypes persist because social segregation still exists in many American communities. People of different races generally have few opportunities to form friendships or to interact with each other in meaningful ways. As a result, people are less inclined to see members of other racial groups as individuals with unique talents and characteristics.

Others argue that certain stereotypes linger because cultures continue to be influenced by the long-held assumptions and attitudes of previous generations. People are exposed to these stereotypical attitudes early in life, and they become a part of a person's outlook on the world even though that person may actually believe that prejudice is wrong. "In America," writes author David K. Shipler,

> a child has only to breathe and listen and watch to accumulate the prejudices that govern ordinary thought. Even without willful intention, with no active effort, a youngster absorbs the images and caricatures surrounding race. Nobody growing up in America can escape the assumptions and expectations that attach themselves to one group or another.[14]

The Media's Reinforcement of Stereotypes

Many people who are concerned about racism maintain that damaging stereotypes are reinforced by the entertainment industry and by the news media. Yale University professor Martin Gilens, who studies racial images in the media, found that while blacks make up 29 percent of the nation's poor, they form 65 percent of the images of the poor on the leading network television news programs. Gilens also discovered that poor African Americans were often portrayed unsympathetically: "The most sympathetic groups of the poor—i.e., the elderly and the working poor—were under-represented and the least sympathetic group—unemployed working-age adults—was over-represented."[15]

Other observers agree that the news media often engage in their own form of racial profiling by associating social problems such as poverty or drug abuse with certain racial groups. In doing so, they argue, the media help to perpetuate the stereotype of minorities as drug dealers, welfare cheats, or gang members. "News media are

Comedian Richard Pryor satirizes the American stereotype of black people as primitive or unintelligent.

not presenting things as they are—but rather as racial fears project them to be,"[16] asserts journalist Mikal Muharrar.

The powerful influence that the media have on the way Americans think about social problems and race has been documented in several surveys. For example, one study focusing on a Los Angeles station's news coverage found that viewers were so used to seeing African American crime suspects that even when a crime report did not specify the race of a suspect, viewers tended to believe that the suspect was black. Another study discovered that television influences children of all races to attribute positive qualities to white characters and negative qualities to minority characters. Surveyed youths themselves reported that "the news media tend to portray African-American and Latino people more negatively than white and Asian people, particularly when the news is about young people."[17]

Media stereotyping is insidious, many argue, because so many Americans rely on television and mainstream newsmagazines as sources of information about current events. When the media portray violence, drug abuse, and criminality as primarily minority problems, the public is more likely to support punitive actions that target minority groups, such as racial profiling in law enforcement. Thus, many observers point out, minorities bear the brunt of public anxiety about enduring social problems.

Stereotypes and Discrimination

Racial minorities are not the only groups that are stereotyped. Whites are also stereotyped by people of color. Some common derogatory stereotypes of whites include the beliefs that they are greedy, cold-hearted, and two-faced. As with the stereotypes of minorities, stereotypes of whites presume that certain negative traits are typically exhibited by white people. These race-based generalizations deny a white person's full humanity and individuality. However, many people argue that because whites constitute the dominant group in the United States, their negative attitudes about racial minorities have more potential for societal harm. Whites in positions of power who harbor the stereotypical beliefs that Latinos are hot-tempered, that Asians are passive, or that blacks are lazy are more likely to deny those minorities opportunities that whites take for granted.

Even whites who believe that they are committed to equal opportunity may be influenced by racial stereotypes, many social analysts point out. Well-intentioned white employers may hesitate to choose an African American job applicant for a sales position, for example, because the employer fears that their patrons will not feel comfortable buying products from a black salesperson. The employer may sincerely believe the applicant is qualified, but worries that the racial stereotypes of their customers will adversely affect sales. Over time, such fears on the part of white employers add up, resulting in large numbers of black candidates being denied certain kinds of jobs.

Ironically, many observers point out, some racial generalizations actually help certain minorities get jobs. Asian Americans, who are commonly stereotyped as diligent, hardworking, and obedient, may find that many employers are eager to hire them. However, because Asians are also stereotyped as passive and socially awkward, employers are not inclined to promote them to higher management-level positions. Thus, many argue, whites continue to be overrepresented in high-status positions that grant them decision-making power and responsibility, while most minorities remain in lower-level jobs.

Over time, the racial discrimination that results from negative stereotypes can create and maintain economic disparities between

A young boy sits on the steps of his home in Tunica County, Mississippi, one of the nation's poorest counties. About 30 percent of black families live in poverty.

different racial groups. Many argue that since minorities do not have the same kind of access that whites have to social, educational, and work opportunities, success is harder for them to achieve. Analysts often point to certain statistics as proof. For instance, about 30 percent of black households currently have incomes below the poverty line in comparison to 8 percent of white households. The average black household income is only half that of the average white household income. In 1993, for every dollar earned by white men, Latino men earned 64 cents. That same year, black women earned 53 cents to every dollar earned by white men.

Many, however, dispute the meaning of these statistics. Despite lingering economic disparities, minorities have continued to advance in American society since the middle of the twentieth century. Some point to the growing black and Hispanic middle class as proof that minorities are in a healthy state of transition. The studies and statistics drawn from one point in time do not reflect such ongoing progress, many commentators argue. Author Linda Chavez maintains that the last few decades of the twentieth century have brought U.S.-born Hispanics greater economic opportunity and social mobility: "Their educational level has been steadily rising, their earnings no longer reflect wide disparities with those of non-Hispanics, and their occupational distribution is coming to resemble more closely that of the general population."[18]

A large percentage of whites do not believe that racial stereotypes and racial discrimination are impediments to minority success today. Numerous polls and surveys reveal that a majority of whites believe that much of the problem of racial intolerance in the United States has been solved. As a 1997 Gallup poll pointed out, "from the white perspective, there are fewer race problems, less discrimination, and abundance of opportunity for blacks, and only minimal personal prejudice." A 1995 *Washington Post* survey, moreover, revealed that only 36 percent of whites believe that "past and present discrimination is a major reason for economic and social problems"[19] facing minorities. Some whites claim that today's racial disparities stem not from discrimination but from personal irresponsibility, individual inadequacies, or poor family values on the part of minorities.

The Daily Experience of Discrimination

Many analysts maintain that such conflicting opinions about discrimination exist because whites rarely see acts of racism while people of color experience them all the time. Minority thinkers and writers often contend that they experience subtle discrimination on a daily basis. One psychologist asserts that, "while whites are generally privileged or given the benefit of the doubt, too often persons of color are simply doubted." [20]

This doubt, many point out, is evident in white people's reactions to people of color. Minorities report that whites are often anxious in their presence: Salesclerks follow them around in stores, worried that they might shoplift something; taxi drivers refuse to give them rides; whites become fearful when they have to stand near black or Latino men in elevators. One black college student describes his evening walk from his job to his apartment in a predominantly white neighborhood as a daily indignity:

> Every day that you live as a black person you're reminded how you're perceived in society. You walk the streets at night; white people cross the streets. I've seen white couples and individuals dart in front of cars to not be on the same side of the street. . . . [When I pass] white men tighten their grip on their women. I've seen people turn around [as if] they're going to take blows from me. The police constantly make circles around me as I walk home. . . . I'll walk, and they'll turn a block. And they'll come around me just to make sure, to find out where I'm going. So, every day you realize [you're black]. Even though you're not doing anything wrong; you're just existing. You're just a person. But you're a black person perceived in an unblack world. [21]

Many Whites Maintain That They Are Not Prejudiced

Whites are often at a loss when they hear of minorities' anxieties about racial discrimination. Many whites do not believe that racial stereotypes influence their own interactions with people of color. Recent surveys report that 85 to 90 percent of U.S. whites believe that they do not harbor any racial prejudices.

Some whites express indignation when confronted with the idea that racial discrimination is still a serious problem for people of color. A white government official, for example, admits that "I get a little upset when I hear black people disagree that [race relations have] come a long way."[22] Some white people also contend that minorities misinterpret relatively harmless incidents, such as being treated rudely by taxi drivers, as examples of prejudice. Since whites themselves encounter negative and rude behavior from other whites in public settings, they often believe that people of color are simply mistaking unmannerly behavior for racism.

Many minorities maintain that they realize that every adverse encounter with whites is not due to racism. But people of color can expend a lot of emotional energy trying to interpret whites' negative actions and comments. Because they do not want to jump to easy conclusions, they may find themselves feeling ambivalent and suspicious in interactions with whites. One commentator details the

Signs like this one were common in the South during the segregation era.

Many Americans feel that racial discrimination has diminished significantly since the days of enforced segregation.

silent questions that minorities might ask themselves: "Was it because of your [color] that you were denied the promotion, excluded from the meeting, treated rudely by the salesclerk, ignored by the professor? Was the unpleasant remark, glance, or laughter an encrypted expression of racial prejudice?"[23] Such attempts to decipher white behavior are exhausting and emotionally draining, many analysts point out. Equally burdensome is the anger that people of color may feel when whites deny that minorities are encountering racial discrimination.

The Need for Dialogue

Understanding the dynamics of prejudice and stereotypes is proving to be a daunting challenge for Americans. Many of those who champion racial justice believe that whites and minorities must openly and respectfully discuss their experiences and their opinions with each other. Such dialogue, maintain diversity consultants Andrea Ayvazian and Beverly Daniel Tatum, could help Americans "move beyond polite and empty words, beyond slogans and accusations, and beyond the fears and hurts that close us off from one another." [24] Carefully planned and organized community discussions on race, many argue, may prove to be the beginning of the end of the racial divide.

Chapter 2

Can America Accept Its Increasing Racial Diversity?

FRANK H. WU, AN AMERICAN citizen of Chinese descent, was born and raised in the Midwest. As a child growing up in Detroit, Michigan, Wu and his family often visited Windsor, Ontario—just a brief trip over the border in Canada—to enjoy good Chinese food. The Canadian border guards would ask some routine questions when the Wus entered Ontario—questions that would be asked of any American citizens crossing over into Canada. But the return trip to the United States, Wu recalls, could be quite a different experience.

In the early 1990s, for example, when Wu was a law student, he visited Canada with three friends—two of them Asian American and one of them white. When they reentered the United States, the U.S. Customs Service detained them, saying they would have to answer a few extra questions. The group was taken to an office and asked where they were born and what they did for a living. For some reason, customs agents inquired further with Wu, asking him how he had met his white friend, how long they had known each other, and what was the nature of their relationship. Apparently satisfied by their answers, the agents then released Wu and his friends. The entire incident lasted just fifteen minutes, and nothing really troubling had occurred.

Afterward, though, Wu wondered if there was a special reason that they had been detained. He also wanted to know why he, and not his white friend, had been asked additional questions. So he wrote a letter of inquiry to the Customs Service.

A month later, a government representative wrote back to him, explaining that law enforcement officials . . . cannot distinguish between honorable, law-abiding citizens and violators on the basis of their physical appearance alone. Many attempts at alien smuggling are made by people posing to be friends [of] a 'non-suspect' traveler. . . . Even though the questions may seem irrelevant or out of place to you, there is a purpose for asking them.[25]

In Wu's opinion, the letter and the incident at the U.S.-Canadian border reveals a racially biased policy. Even though both he and his white friend had proof of U.S. citizenship, spoke the same language, and wore similar clothing, officials grew suspicious simply because Wu was of Chinese descent and one of his traveling partners was white. In other words, an assumption about possible alien smuggling was made largely on the basis of Wu's racial "difference": his Asian features. A group of white Americans traveling together would not have aroused this kind of suspicion, Wu contends, even if one of them had been born outside the United States.

The customs officials treated Wu in a civil manner and did not intend any insult. However, Wu believes that his experience illuminates a much larger problem. The citizenship of nonwhites, particularly Asians and Latinos, is often questioned. The citizenship of whites, though, is rarely doubted. This reasoning equates "whiteness" with "American-ness" and reinforces the notion that nonwhites are outsiders, foreigners, and "aliens." In Wu's opinion, this kind of thinking creates an "us-versus-them" mentality in which whites are seen as trustworthy while minorities, particularly Asians and Latinos, are considered suspicious. Such thinking reveals a hidden assumption that the United States is a Caucasian country—a place where whites are entitled to live—when in fact it is a nation comprising many races and ethnicities.

The Changing Face of America

Wu's opinions are especially pertinent in light of the changes taking place in America's racial and ethnic makeup. The U.S. Census Bureau predicts that by the year 2050, the numbers of Hispanic and Asian Americans will increase significantly while the number of whites will decrease until they make up about half of the nation's population. The percentage of Hispanics, for example, will increase from 10.2 percent to 24.5 percent, and the Asian population will increase from 3.3 percent to 8.2 percent. In the meantime, the percentage of whites in the population will decrease from 74 percent to 53 percent, and the black population will remain fairly stable, rising from 12 percent to 13.6 percent by the middle of the twenty-first century.

Many analysts contend that this population shift will be as dramatic as the changes that occurred when the slave trade transformed the racial makeup of the South. "The world is not going to be the same in 30 years as it is now,"[26] says Gregory Spencer, director of the Population Projections Branch at the Census Bureau. In some places, such as California, there will no longer be a majority race—a fact that will make the term *minority* obsolete in that state.

The term minority *may hold less significance in the future as the percentage of Americans of color increases and the percentage of whites decreases.*

Will the United States Become a "Balkanized" Nation?

Some experts worry that the higher birthrates among Asian and Hispanic Americans, along with an increase in immigration from Asia and Latin America, will threaten the nation's ability to manage its population. They fear that the United States will eventually be gripped by dangerous racial and socioeconomic conflicts as competing ethnic groups fight to promote their own interests at the expense of all others. If this happens, these analysts maintain, the United States will become a fragmented nation—a young democracy thwarted by barriers of culture, language, and race.

Many observers charge that such fears are rooted in racial prejudice and ignorance. They maintain that people who lack knowledge about cultures other than their own tend to fear changes that might bring them, or their group, into contact with other races and ethnicities. Those who operate on the assumption that different cultures are unable to peacefully coexist seem to have the most anxieties about America's upcoming population changes, these observers point out.

However, several social analysts insist that anxieties about cultural disintegration are not the result of ignorance or racism but are instead based on an understanding of world history and current events. The nations in Eurasia and Africa, for example, witnessed numerous interethnic wars throughout the twentieth century. During the late twentieth and early twenty-first centuries, the Balkan Peninsula countries of Yugoslavia, Romania, and Albania have experienced such notorious interethnic hostilities that the word *balkanized* is now commonly used to describe regions torn apart by ethnic conflicts. The United States has no reason to consider itself immune to balkanization, experts argue.

On the other hand, many other critics contend that their concerns about America's changing population are economic rather than racial and cultural. They believe that a growing number of immigrants—particularly illegal immigrants—could strain the U.S. economy. Some politicians maintain that since immigrants create a large labor pool and settle for lower pay, they take jobs from U.S.-born workers and drive down the wages of citizens who retain their jobs. Many also believe that illegal immigrants are a drain on social benefits such as welfare, health care, and education—benefits that should be reserved for U.S. citizens. These economic worries are often cited as the main reason why many Americans support strict immigration control measures.

Some analysts, though, believe that the economic focus on legal and illegal immigrants has racial overtones. For one thing, argue professors Timothy Tseng and David Yoo, "negative stereotypes of 'job-stealing immigrants' and the 'welfare mom' are employed regularly to justify immigration restrictions." They also maintain that even positive images of successful, hardworking immigrants are used to silence complaints that racial discrimination remains a problem: "Asian-American educational and economic 'success' stories, for instance, are often used to exhort [other minorities] to 'stop whining!' "[27] Those who agree with Tseng and Yoo contend that concerned community leaders must avoid stigmatizing immigrants or pitting immigrants of color against U.S.-born minorities.

Some critics assert that successful Asian Americans are held up as evidence to disprove that racial discrimination is still prevalent.

A Different Outlook on Race Relations

Some people are optimistic about the upcoming population changes, noting that the United States has always been a nation of immigrants and descendants of immigrants. These optimists have hopes that Americans will embrace the country's increasing diversity and build communities based on shared values, economic justice, and respect for differences. If this comes to pass, they argue, the United States will persevere as the world's first truly multiracial democracy. In a 1997 speech President Bill Clinton expressed confidence about a future rich in cultural variety: "The diverse backgrounds and talents of our citizens can help America to light the globe, showing nations deeply divided by race, religion and tribe that there is a better way."[28]

For this to happen, Americans will have to exert considerable effort to combat the effects of racial and cultural prejudice. Most analysts remain uncertain, though, about how willing most people are to confront and challenge deeply ingrained biases.

There are certainly many factors to consider as the United States undergoes the shift in its racial and ethnic makeup. Adjusting to the changes will require a different outlook on race relations. For much of U.S. history, investigations of racial conflict have concentrated on the relationship between black and white Americans. This is because African Americans have long made up the largest minority group in the country, and tensions between the white majority and the black minority have dominated debates about racism and race relations. However, as Latinos replace African Americans as the largest minority group, relations between Anglos and Latinos are likely to command more attention. Interactions between the various minority groups—and the growing population of mixed-race people—will also revise popular notions of race relations as America becomes inhabited by more residents of color.

The Debate over Illegal Immigration

Illegal immigration is one of the most controversial topics tied into the larger issue of America's increasing diversity. In addition, current debates over illegal immigration reveal yet another aspect of the disagreement whites and minorities have concerning racially charged issues. While a majority of whites support restrictions on illegal immigration, people of color tend to be much more ambivalent about anti-immigration measures.

The 1990s controversy over illegal immigration in California provides a revealing example of this difference of opinion. Because it borders Mexico, California has a large number of illegal residents—some experts estimate hundreds of thousands. Most of them are Mexican nationals working menial jobs to support their families or to find a way out of poverty. These Latino immigrants, often referred to as "undocumented workers" or "illegal aliens," cross the border to live in camps or inexpensive housing in southern California's Latino

In the hills between San Diego, California, and Tijuana, Mexico, U.S. Border Patrol agents arrest immigrants attempting to enter the United States illegally.

communities. Some of them are migrant farm laborers; others take jobs as housekeepers, food service workers, hotel maids, or factory workers.

In 1994 California governor Pete Wilson took a strong stance against illegal immigration, asking the federal government to adopt stricter policies to secure the U.S.-Mexico border. Many Californians supported Wilson's efforts, agreeing that illegal immigrants from Mexico were becoming a strain on the state's educational, medical, and law enforcement resources. In 1994, for example, illegal immigrants were 14 percent of California's total prison population. Two-thirds of all babies born in Los Angeles public hospitals were born to undocumented immigrants, and California was spending $1.7 billion each year to educate students known to be living in the country illegally. These statistics, Wilson argued, revealed a crisis in immigration that was making "a mockery of our laws. It is a slap in the face to the tens of thousands who play by the rules and endure the arduous process of legally immigrating to our country. It's time to restore reason, integrity, and fairness to our nation's immigration policy." [29]

Several other politicians who agreed with Wilson started a "Save Our State" coalition, which resulted in Proposition 187, a ballot measure that would deny illegal immigrants the use of nonemergency public health services and public education. The measure would require employees of public agencies—including doctors, nurses, and teachers—to report any person they suspected of being in the country illegally.

In the 1994 California Voter Information Pamphlet, the authors of Proposition 187 discussed the need for economic fairness for California's taxpaying legal residents:

It has been estimated that ILLEGAL ALIENS are costing taxpayers in excess of 5 billion dollars a year.

While our own citizens and legal residents go wanting, those who choose to enter our country ILLEGALLY get royal treatment at the expense of the California taxpayer. . . .

Should our children's classrooms be over-crowded by those who are ILLEGALLY in our country? . . .

Should tax-paid bureaucrats be able to give sanctuary to those ILLEGALLY in our country?

If your answer to these questions is NO, then you should support Proposition 187.[30]

A Racist Proposition?

Critics of Proposition 187 charged that the emphasis on the words *illegal* and *alien* revealed its authors' intent to demonize and dehumanize undocumented immigrants. (Many people are offended by the word *alien*, because it suggests that an individual is a nonhuman from another planet instead of a person from another country.) If the proposition became law, critics argued, it would promote a climate of suspicion and discrimination against all immigrants—who are usually people of color—and stigmatize anyone who appeared or sounded foreign.

California governor Pete Wilson advocated stricter policies for illegal immigrants.

Many also maintained that the proposition made scapegoats out of California's Latinos, wrongly blaming them for the state's economic woes. This misplaced blame, analysts pointed out, could be seen in two troubling facts connected with Proposition 187. One was that California's illegal Latino immigrants were largely employed by Anglos, the group that was apparently most supportive of the immigration-control measure. Critics claimed that Anglos seeking out cheap labor deserved much of the blame for making California attractive to undocumented workers.

Another unsettling truth bearing on Proposition 187 was the fact that American Indians and Mexicans inhabited California long before Anglos did. As Latino writer Aaron Gallegos notes, "In the beginning, it was not Latinos who migrated to this nation, but this nation that migrated to our lands. The failure to recognize this has resulted in policies and images that treat Hispanics as if they are in some way 'alien' to the United States."[31] In Gallegos's view, the drive to bar "illegal aliens" from the United States shows that many whites see themselves as entitled to be American residents but perceive Latinos and other immigrants of color—whether legal or illegal—as outsiders and troublemakers. He believes that a more civil approach to the immigration issue would acknowledge the needs of both Anglos and Latinos.

Polls and the 1994 California Election

A majority of U.S. citizens, however, claim to be rather sympathetic to the plight of immigrants and illegal immigrants. Surveys reveal that just 20 percent of Americans believe that immigrants take jobs from citizens; 69 percent believe that immigrants do work that U.S. citizens will not do. Only a small minority claims that the American-born children of illegal immigrants should be denied public education.

Nevertheless, in 1994 California voters approved Proposition 187, and exit polls revealed that non-Hispanic whites, who made up most of the electorate, were largely responsible for the measure's initial success: 63 percent of white voters approved the proposition, while it was rejected by 77 percent of Latino voters and 53 percent of Asian and black voters.

Most Anglos who supported the proposition insisted that their vote was based on economic, not racial, concerns. Many of them approve of any immigration that is legal and that does not overtax state and government resources. "I'm the grandchild of immigrants," California governor Pete Wilson stated in a 1994 speech.

> My grandmother came to this country in steerage from Ireland at age 16. . . . And America benefited from her and millions like her. But we, as a sovereign nation, have a right and an obligation to determine how and when people come to our country. We are a nation of laws, and people who seek to be a part of this great nation must do so according to the law.[32]

Many white and minority thinkers, however, believe that voter approval of Proposition 187 was at least partly based on aversion to racial diversity. Population researcher William Frey, for example, conducted a study that revealed that U.S. citizens, particularly working-class whites, were leaving regions that had received a large influx of Asian and Latin American immigrants in the 1980s and 1990s. Frey analyzed the movement of populations in the ten major cities that received the most immigrants during those decades. He discovered that between 1985 and 1995, more than 5 million immigrants moved to those cities; during that same time, about 4.5 million existing residents moved away. According to the American Immigration Control Foundation, the residents who leave not only want to avoid job competition and other economic woes, they also want to move to "a community with a lot of other people [who are] racially and ethnically like themselves."[33]

A few whites openly admit that they do not wish to live alongside increasing populations of Latino and Asian Americans, especially those who are recent immigrants. Journalist Jared Taylor, for instance, states that "the folkways, the demeanor and the texture of life that whites take for granted cannot survive the embrace of large numbers of aliens."[34] Those who agree with Taylor fear that European American culture is in danger of being eclipsed by minority immigrant cultures and that a once-unified nation will soon become characterized by battling ethnic enclaves: "There is not one multi-racial

anything in America that doesn't suffer from racial friction. . . .
Diversity of race or tribe or language or religion are the main reasons people are at each other's throats all around the world. Just pick
up a newspaper. Diversity—within the same territory—is strife, not
strength."[35] Although only a minority of citizens openly acknowl-
edges such sentiments about diversity, some observers maintain that
these fears are more prevalent than most Americans are willing to
admit.

What Became of Proposition 187?

California's Proposition 187 never went into effect. In 1998 federal
judge Mariana Pfaelzer declared it unconstitutional, citing a 1982
Supreme Court ruling that all children under age eighteen—regardless of their immigration status—are entitled to public education.
Although backers of the proposition initially pushed for further
appeals, the state's newly elected governor, Gray Davis, decided to
abandon efforts to implement the measure.

Many Californians, particularly Latinos, welcomed Davis's
decision, as did a number of advocacy groups that had organized to
fight Proposition 187. One of these groups, the Californians for Justice, noted that the denial of public benefits to undocumented immigrants would have affected all Californians regardless of citizenship
status. Denial of health care to illegal residents, for example, could
have resulted in an overall increase in infectious disease. Denial of
public education to immigrant children could have resulted in more
illiteracy, poverty, crime, and social disintegration.

For many, these insights about the defunct proposition show that
what affects one segment of the U.S. population will eventually
affect the whole. For this reason, new ideas and policies must be
viewed in light of how they will impact all residents—legal and illegal, white and minority. This idea is summed up by Mexican American artist and activist Guillermo Gomez-Pena:

> It is time to face the facts: Anglos won't go back to Europe,
> and Mexicans and Latinos (legal or illegal) won't go back to
> Latin America. We are all here to stay. For better or for worse,
> our destinies are in one another's hands. . . . Rather than more

border patrols, border walls, and punitive laws, we need more and better information about one another. . . . We need to educate our children and teenagers about the dangers of racism and the complexities of living in a multiracial borderless society, the inevitable society of the twenty-first century.[36]

Culturally Inclusive Education

Many experts agree with Gomez-Pena that the best preparation for the upcoming shift in America's population is education, particularly education that reflects the nation's racial and ethnic diversity. Too often, educators point out, students go to school with negative stereotypes and misconceptions about people of different races. If these misconceptions are not addressed and challenged in the classroom, prejudiced attitudes can become ingrained and ethnic and racial divisions deepen.

California governor Gray Davis announces the end of Proposition 187.

One reason why racial prejudice has persisted, many observers point out, is because too many U.S. schools have focused on the contributions of white Europeans and white Americans when teaching science, literature, and history. The contributions of people of color, however, have often been omitted or minimized—so much so that many students end up concluding that modern civilization is solely the product of European men and their descendants.

Most students, for example, are familiar with such names as Paul Revere, the American Revolutionary War hero; Meriwether Lewis and William Clark, famed explorers of the American West; and Jonas Salk, the inventor of the polio vaccine. Not as many would recognize such names as Crispus Attucks, the runaway slave who was the first to die in the attack that spurred the American Revolution; Sacagawea, the Shoshone Native American woman who served as interpreter and guide for the Lewis and Clark expedition; or Onesimus, the black slave who developed the concept of inoculation and vaccination in the 1700s.

When students receive lessons that praise the accomplishments of whites but ignore the contributions and perspectives of people of color, schools reinforce damaging stereotypes of minorities as inferior and insignificant, experts argue. To remedy this, many educators have promoted "culturally inclusive" education—an education that recognizes the racially and culturally diverse influences in history, the arts, and the sciences. According to the New York State Education Task Force on Minorities, such an education would serve "the interests of all children from all cultures: children from minority cultures will have higher self-esteem and self-respect, while children from European cultures will have a less arrogant perspective of being part of the group that has 'done it all.'"[37]

Does Inclusive Education Ignore the Facts?

Critics, on the other hand, maintain that culturally inclusive education sounds good in theory but often fails in practice. They argue that the most important lessons for both white and minority students involve the basic skills of reading, writing, and math. Inclusive education deemphasizes these basic skills in order to give students more time to learn about cultural diversity, these critics contend.

Crispus Attucks, the first American colonist to die in the Boston Massacre of 1770.

Some analysts claim, moreover, that culturally inclusive education presents a distortion of history. In a misguided attempt to improve minority self-esteem, critics argue, multicultural educators too often ignore the negative events in minority histories and omit the positive achievements of Europeans and white Americans. In reviewing discussions of slavery in several current textbooks, historian Alvin J. Schmidt notes that

> they consistently ignore the practice of slavery in non-Western cultures. For example, textbooks say nothing about the many American Indian tribes who practiced slavery long before Columbus and other Europeans came to America. . . . Slavery is a moral evil, and that fact does not change, regardless of what group practiced it. . . . [Textbooks] need to emphasize that it is evil in every society and not just in American culture.[38]

Critics strongly agree with Schmidt that students should not be led to conclude that only whites, and not minorities, are capable of committing atrocities. While many grant that an increased awareness of minority contributions to history is an important goal, some fear that certain kinds of multicultural education promote a dangerously incomplete picture of history.

Valuing the Real America

Most U.S. teachers, however, maintain that a true education not only gives students basic skills but also bequeaths to them a genuine appreciation of what it means to live in a society characterized by racial and cultural variety. Many believe that if a healthy percentage of schools adopt well-planned inclusive education, young people will learn to respect, even value, the ideas of those of different races and ethnicities. If this comes to pass, more future leaders will have the skills to help bridge racial divides and unify a richly diverse and growing nation.

Chapter 3

Does Affirmative Action Counteract Racial Discrimination?

ACH YEAR THE UNIVERSITY OF CALIFORNIA at Berkeley admits a little more than eight hundred students to its prestigious law school. In the fall of 1996, seventy-five black students were newly enrolled—representing about 9 percent of all new Berkeley law students that year. But just one year later, in 1997, only fifteen new African American law students were admitted.

Many believe that this sudden drop in black enrollment—noticed at several California universities in 1997—was a foreseeable result of Proposition 209, a ballot measure approved by California voters in 1996. Also known as the California Civil Rights Initiative, this measure ended affirmative action programs in state hiring and public university admissions. Previously, affirmative action policies had required the state of California to ensure minority representation in its workforce and college populations by including race and gender as factors in hiring and college admissions decisions. But in 1996 a majority of California voters decided that affirmative action programs were discriminatory against whites, and they were ready to adopt a new measure declaring that the state could not discriminate against or grant preferential treatment to any individual or group on the basis of race, sex, color, ethnicity, or national origin in the operation of public employment, education, and contracting.

Today's affirmative action debate, for the most part, focuses on racial discrimination, particularly discrimination against African

Americans. This is because the status of African Americans has been the subject of much of the controversy and legislation involving race in the United States. In fact, affirmative action arose out of the civil rights struggle of the 1950s and 1960s—a movement that sought to end state-sponsored discrimination against blacks.

As early as 1953, the Presidential Committee on Government Contract Compliance advised the Bureau of Employment Security to act "affirmatively to implement the policy of nondiscrimination." But the phrase *affirmative action* was not coined until 1961, when President John Kennedy created the Equal Employment Opportunity Commission (EEOC) and urged contractors working on federally funded projects to "take affirmative action to ensure that applicants are employed without regard to race, creed, color or national origin."[39] Kennedy's directive was strengthened by the Civil Rights Act of 1964, which banned racial discrimination in the workplace and in public accommodations.

President John F. Kennedy coined the phrase affirmative action.

(Left to right) Reverend Jesse Jackson, San Francisco supervisor Mabel Teng, and San Francisco mayor Willie Brown lead a march across the Golden Gate Bridge to support affirmative action.

In 1965 President Lyndon Johnson ordered the enforcement of guidelines aimed to eliminate racial imbalance in hiring policies. In 1972 Congress passed the Equal Employment Opportunity Act, which allowed citizens to file lawsuits against companies with discriminatory hiring practices. In 1975 the Supreme Court ruled that achieving a discrimination-free workplace could require companies to consider race as a factor when hiring new employees. And in 1980 the Supreme Court upheld the practice of setting aside 10 percent of public works contracts for businesses owned by minorities.

Types of Affirmative Action

Law professor Paul Butler asserts that affirmative action has three different goals. One is to remedy past discrimination, "to put ethnic minorities . . . where they would be, had the discrimination never occurred."[40] The second objective is to compensate for ongoing discrimination, and the third aim is racial diversity—particularly diversity in the workforce.

To achieve these objectives, two basic types of affirmative action have been adopted: process-oriented policies and goal-oriented policies.

In the world of work, process-oriented policies ensure that job openings are advertised widely so that all interested white and minority persons have a chance to apply. Employers might also take advantage of outreach and recruitment programs that help to enlarge the minority applicant pool.

Process-oriented policies, moreover, focus on fair and nondiscriminatory treatment of all applicants—each must be given the same skills tests, evaluations, and interview questions. Ideally, author and educator Beverly Daniel Tatum points out, "The [job] search committee can freely choose the 'best' candidate knowing that no discrimination has taken place. Under such circumstances, the 'best' candidate will sometimes be a person of color."[41] Because it emphasizes commonly held democratic ideas of equal opportunity and fairness, a majority of Americans, both white and minority, support process-oriented affirmative action.

Goal-oriented affirmative action goes one step further than process-oriented affirmative action: Once an employer has found a pool of qualified applicants, individuals whose race will help the company reach its diversity objectives are favored. The person who gets the job will not always be a minority, but minorities are granted "extra points" during the employer's decision-making process. Today many Americans are critical of goal-oriented affirmative action because they believe it results in unfair preferences for minorities and discrimination against whites—often referred to as "reverse discrimination." For this reason, goal-oriented policies are the focus of the current debate about affirmative action.

Affirmative Action Rollbacks

From the mid-1960s through the mid-1970s, most of the legislation surrounding affirmative action emphasized the need to take aggressive steps to achieve racial diversity in workplaces and educational institutions. But from the late 1970s through the 1990s, lawmakers began to limit the scope of affirmative action. Many observers argue that the late 1970s court case *Regents of the University of California v. Bakke* was a turning point in affirmative action history. The case involved Allan Bakke, a college student who claimed that the University of California at Davis denied him admission to its medical school because he was white. Bakke's lawyers maintained that the medical school's practice of retaining a certain number of slots for minority students discriminated against qualified white students. The case went to the Supreme Court, which ruled that colleges may consider race in admissions decisions but may not set aside a fixed number of slots for minorities. Thus, the use of affirmative action quotas in hiring and college admissions was banned.

Several Supreme Court decisions in the 1980s and 1990s continued to limit the scope of affirmative action. For instance, in 1995 the Court struck down a decision in which a white contractor's low

Allan Bakke believed that the University of California denied him admission because of his race.

bid on a city construction project was rejected in favor of a Hispanic contractor's higher bid. The Hispanic contractor's bid had originally been accepted on affirmative action grounds as part of a policy requiring a certain percentage of public works projects to be given to minority-owned contracting firms. Although the Court had upheld such policies in 1980, its 1995 decision maintained that "equal protection of the law is a personal right, not a group right. Laws classifying citizens by race pose a great threat to that right."[42]

In 1997 the Supreme Court declined to review an appeals court decision favoring California's Proposition 209—a decision that allowed the anti–affirmative action measure to stand. The success of the California initiative has encouraged several other states to place anti–affirmative action measures on their ballots.

The Concerns of Affirmative Action Supporters

Many people are distressed about these rollbacks, arguing that affirmative action programs remain necessary because discrimination still exists in America and its institutions. In their opinion, affirmative action is one of the best ways to ensure equal opportunity in education and employment for minorities. Much of the social and economic success that people of color have achieved since the 1960s, many point out, is due to affirmative action. As Hilary O. Shelton, an acting director of the National Association for the Advancement of Colored People (NAACP), argues, affirmative action was responsible for the increase in black enrollment at U.S. colleges during the latter half of the twentieth century:

> In 1955, only 4.9 percent of college students ages 18–24 was African American. . . . Only in the wake of affirmative action measures in the late 1960s and early 70s did the percentage of black college students begin to climb steadily: In 1970, 7.8 percent of college students were African American, in 1980, 9.1 percent, and in 1990, 11.3 percent.[43]

Other statistics attest to the beneficial results of affirmative action. Several key U.S. industries, for example, have seen an increase in black participation. Between 1970 and 1990, the number of black electricians grew from 14,145 to 43,276; bank tellers, from

10,633 to 46,332; health officials, from 3,914 to 13,235; and pharmacists, from 2,501 to 7,011. Such dramatic changes would not have occurred without goal-oriented affirmative action, its supporters contend.

Although affirmative action has contributed significantly to minority gains during the past three decades, many proponents believe that it is just as necessary today as it was in the 60s and 70s. Analysts often point out that people of color still face discriminatory barriers in jobs and education. According to a 1998 study conducted by the Fair Employment Council and Urban Institute, black and Hispanic job applicants encounter discrimination once in every five times they apply for a job. Furthermore, the Federal Glass Ceiling Commission reports that 97 percent of senior managers at the top

The number of black pharmacists in the United States nearly tripled between 1970 and 1990.

U.S. industrial corporations are white males, yet they make up only 43 percent of the workforce. Recent statistics also reveal that African American men with a college degree earn as much as $15,180 less than their white counterparts.

The discrimination that people of color face in the job market is often so subtle, affirmative action supporters maintain, that only policies that aggressively seek out minorities can counteract it. Many whites, for example, have unfettered access to education and employment due to family ties, school connections, and personal referral networks that minorities usually lack. Preferential hiring of minorities, many contend, is the best way to correct the ongoing injustices that have resulted from decades of preferential hiring of whites.

The Concerns of Affirmative Action Critics

The majority of affirmative action critics have concerns about goal-oriented policies and programs. Generally, these critics commend laws that ban racial discrimination against minorities in hiring and education. They also support process-oriented affirmative action measures intended to enlarge the minority applicant pool. But these critics argue that the use of any racial preferences in employment or college admissions is a form of discrimination that thwarts the ideals of equal opportunity and fairness. In the opinion of Roger Clegg, general counsel of the Center for Equal Opportunity, "You can't undo the discrimination against some blacks by some whites in the past by requiring new discrimination on behalf of different blacks against different whites. The solution to the discrimination that exists is not more discrimination. It is to enforce the laws we have and to stop discriminating."[44]

Goal-oriented affirmative action, these critics maintain, requires employers to make plans about how many minorities they must hire to achieve a certain standard of diversity. This practice, many contend, amounts to no more than the establishment of racial quotas, or the setting aside of a predetermined number of positions for people of color. Although the Supreme Court decision in the *Bakke* case was supposed to have made quotas illegal, the setting of explicit goals for minority hiring creates de facto (existing but illegal) quotas, many analysts point out.

Quotas Versus Goals

On occasion, federal courts may order certain organizations to employ "consent decrees." Consent decrees are temporary quotas imposed on institutions that have a well-documented record of blatant discrimination. Because such institutions are in violation of the

Demonstrators protest Allan Bakke's case in 1977. The Supreme Court ruled that colleges may consider race in admissions, but may not set racial quotas.

Civil Rights Act, the government can require them to hire a certain percentage of minorities. In 1987, for instance, the San Francisco Fire Department was issued a consent decree that boosted the number of blacks in officer positions from seven to thirty-one, the number of Hispanic officers from twelve to fifty-five, and Asians from zero to ten.

Legal quotas, which are rare, exist only in the province of civil rights law enforcement. Goal-oriented affirmative action programs, however, are often mistaken for quotas. Many claim that confusion about the difference between a goal and a quota is at the root of many arguments against affirmative action. While temporary quotas can only be imposed by court order, goals involve an organization's voluntary decision to increase minority representation. Such goals do not entail the allotting of a specific number of positions for minorities. Their purpose, analysts maintain, is to give an organization something to reach for in its aim for diversity. Unlike quotas, goals are flexible, can be revised, and do not shut out whites seeking coveted positions, affirmative action supporters contend.

But critics often maintain that de facto quotas are more common than affirmative action supporters are willing to admit. Furthermore, even if rigid quotas are rarely used, racial preferences often are. Such preferences are just as discriminatory against whites as are quotas, critics assert. And many argue that the existence of preferences increases tensions between whites and minorities, who often disagree about the nature of affirmative action.

A Cycle of Misunderstandings

Leonard Steinhorn and Barbara Diggs-Brown, the authors of *By the Color of Our Skin*, maintain that affirmative action and other attempts to remedy discrimination make the racial-perception gap especially noticeable. In their opinion, a chain reaction of racial misunderstandings begins when whites claim that discrimination is no longer a serious problem in America. The more whites deny the existence of racial discrimination, the more blacks and other minorities feel compelled to insist that it still occurs. "To the white ear that makes black demands seem strident and aggressive, which then reinforces the white view that blacks are complaining,"[45] Steinhorn and Diggs-Brown point out.

Whites who see no evidence of discrimination, furthermore, will conclude that any use of racial preferences is unfair—and will see minorities as receiving special treatment at the expense of whites. As Steinhorn and Diggs-Brown state,

> To whites, "special treatment" . . . conveys a message of injustice and runs contrary to the long-held American belief that people should be treated as individuals, not as members of a group. To blacks, the white inability to acknowledge the prevalence of discrimination is reason enough why affirmative action should continue.[46]

Recent surveys lend support to these authors' claims. Opinion polls taken in the 1990s indicate that between 60 and 75 percent of whites oppose affirmative action, while 65 to 70 percent of minorities support it. Moreover, 60 percent of whites feel that affirmative action discriminates against whites; however, 66 percent of blacks do not believe that they have as good a chance as whites to get any kind of job for which they are qualified.

Why Whites and Minorities Often Disagree About Affirmative Action

A large percentage of whites believes that people of color now have the same opportunities that whites have to obtain jobs, housing, and education. For this reason, many whites argue that it is time to revise, limit, or end affirmative action policies. In their opinion, affirmative action creates preferences that too often favor minorities at the expense of whites. According to Steven Yates, author of *Civil Wrongs: What Went Wrong with Affirmative Action,* "While such ideals as equal employment opportunity sound good in principle, in practice they have come to conceal equally unjust, equally harmful, and probably unconstitutional practices that give preference to some at the expense of others."[47]

Many minorities, on the other hand, feel that racial discrimination still presents barriers to their educational and economic success. Affirmative action, they maintain, is a way to remedy discrimination against people of color by eliminating the unfair advantage that whites enjoyed in the past and still enjoy today.

NAACP chair Julian Bond uses the scenario of a rigged football game to illustrate the need to address unfair white advantage:

> The white team and the black team are playing the last football game of the season. The white team owns the ball, the stadium, and the referees and has been allowed to field nine times as many players. For almost four quarters, the white team has cheated on every play, and now the score is white team 140, black team 3. There are 10 seconds left in the game. Suddenly, the white quarterback feels he must make amends for misdeeds committed before he joined the team. "How about it, boys," he says to his teammates. "From now on, let's play fair!"[48]

"Playing fair," in Bond's opinion, would require measures that place black players at a distinct advantage simply to make up for the lack of advantage they had endured for most of the game.

Julian Bond compared the advantage whites have held throughout the nation's history to a rigged football game.

The Question of Merit

Critics who do not believe that racial preferences are fair often contend that unqualified minorities are granted jobs and college admissions at the expense of more qualified whites. In other words, critics argue, affirmative action policies give minorities positions simply because of their race and not on the basis of skills and merit.

Many affirmative action critics point to a situation at the University of Texas Law School as recent proof that qualified whites have lost coveted positions for the benefit of less-qualified minorities. Four white college students sued the law school in 1992, claiming that they had been denied admission so that less-qualified blacks and Mexican Americans could attend the school. As a result of this suit (*Hopwood v. Texas*), the school was required to reveal the entrance exam scores of its 1992 admittees. The average score of the five hundred new students was 162 (on a scale of 120 to 180), which placed them in the eighty-ninth percentile. The average score for the black students, however, was 158, putting them in the seventy-eighth percentile.

The University of Texas claimed that if only grades and test scores had been considered, only nine blacks instead of forty-one would have been admitted and only eighteen Latinos instead of fifty-five. In effect, to attain a certain level of racial diversity, the law school had been using separate admission standards for white and minority students. Minority students with lower test scores were being admitted to the detriment of some white students with higher scores. This, the lawsuit maintained, was reverse discrimination.

Is True Merit Measurable?

Affirmative action supporters contend, however, that merit must not be defined solely by grades or test scores. If merit were to be based on such standards, only people who have the highest test scores would be granted the most desired positions. But several studies have found that high test scores are not a predictor of an individual's future career success. There are many unmeasurable traits that help make a good lawyer: an ability to overcome adversity, creative capacities, previous business experience, an eagerness to volunteer and serve others, concern for the poor and vulnerable, speaking skills, and several other "untestable" qualities. Test scores should be only one out of many criteria for selecting students, affirmative action supporters maintain.

Others point out that it is unfair to demand that minorities achieve the highest test scores to gain entrance to certain universities. Because of ongoing societal discrimination, many minorities have not had the same access that whites have had to quality education in grade school and high school. For this reason, minority scores on college-entrance exams are, on the whole, slightly lower than those of white students. Affirmative action intends to remedy this situation by taking into consideration the educational disadvantages many people of color have faced. The use of race as a factor in college admissions is an attempt to balance these inequities. As author David K. Shipler asks,

> How shameful can it be, after generations of imprisonment in inferior educational systems, to score lower on a standardized test? How unfair can it be, after three hundred years of white advantage, to spend thirty years redressing the imbalance? And how unwise can it be . . . to search affirmatively past the sterile test scores into a rich human potential not easily measured?[49]

Minority students take the SAT. A career enrichment program provides up to $2,000 with a score of 1,000.

Does Affirmative Action Harm Minorities?

Some critics, both white and minority, feel it is unwise to use race as a factor in hiring and college admissions because it is psychologically harmful to people of color. They contend that affirmative action fosters self-doubt among blacks and Latinos by implying that they succeed only with the help of race-based preferences. Furthermore, critics point out, the existence of preferences leads whites to believe that minorities get desired positions only because of their race. As black affirmative action opponent Ward Connerly puts it,

> Ask the high-achieving black or Chicano student who works hard and gains entry to college solely on the basis of his merit, but who then must endure the nagging question of whether he was admitted because of affirmative action. . . . Ask him whether he thinks it's fair that his accomplishments are devalued.[50]

Preference supporters, on the other hand, maintain that affirmative action always seeks out qualified people. The notion that unqualified minorities are getting positions over qualified whites is rooted in the stereotype that blacks and Latinos are inferior to whites, many analysts argue. This stereotype would exist whether or not affirmative action policies were eliminated. Besides, argues black law professor Paul Butler, "most people who are the beneficiaries of affirmative action do not report feeling [any] stigma"[51] that leads them to doubt their own abilities.

Do Government and Business Have a Responsibility to Promote Diversity?

In the case of *Hopwood v. Texas*, the University of Texas argued that it needed to use racial preferences to correct racial imbalances in the student body. A regional court of appeals ruled that the state had no compelling justification for fostering racial diversity and could not be allowed to elevate some races over others in its admissions policy. As with California's Proposition 209, the Supreme Court declined to hear a further appeal of the *Hopwood* case. This allowed the lower court's decision to stand, which ended the use of affirmative action for universities in several southern states.

In the year following the final decision on the *Hopwood* case, minority enrollment dropped sharply at many prestigious colleges in the South, as was the case in California after Proposition 209 went into effect. Some experts are concerned that the lack of minority representation on these campuses will create a stagnant learning environment that does not reflect the increasing diversity of the outside world.

Diversity in American institutions and businesses is strength, many argue. An organization that hires workers of various backgrounds, for example, is usually better informed about different points of view and has more to offer to its clientele. A 1994 study by the U.S. Department of Labor, moreover, concluded that companies with the best affirmative action records have the highest profits. "In an increasingly multicultural nation with a global reach," one law school dean insists, "a commitment to diversity—to broadening the boundaries of inclusiveness of American institutions—is economically necessary [and] morally imperative."[52]

Affirmative action opponents, however, do not feel that the drop in minority enrollments at selective colleges is a real cause for concern. They point out that the overall college enrollment of blacks and Latinos in California and Texas has remained stable in the 1990s. There has simply been a shift in which campuses minorities attend. For example, a Latino student in California who would have been admitted to the prestigious Berkeley campus under affirmative action may now end up at the San Diego campus—a good, but less selective, college. Many experts believe that the lack of racial preferences will actually boost minority college graduation rates in Texas and California. This is because colleges will only be accepting students capable of doing well in their particular programs, they point out.

Affirmative action critics argue that the best way to foster diversity in American institutions is not to enforce racial preferences but rather to remedy the social problems in minority families and communities. According to Roger Clegg, many people of color are not prepared to compete for coveted positions "because of deteriorating family structure and [poor] public schools. Better to address these problems directly, rather than sweep them under the rug."[53] When more minorities have stable family lives and high-quality education from an early age, Clegg argues, more of them will skillfully compete for any position they desire—with no need for racial preferences.

A Continuing Controversy

Affirmative action is likely to provoke heated debate in the years to come. The success of California's Proposition 209 and the *Hopwood v. Texas* decision have set the stage for other states to call into question their own race-based hiring and college admissions policies. The question of equal opportunity and affirmative action may prove to be one of the most difficult challenges for those seeking the fairest way to close the racial divide.

Chapter 4

How Can Society Curtail Racism?

I<small>N</small> 1997, Tony P. Hall, a white democratic representative from Ohio, submitted a bill in the House of Representatives proposing that Congress apologize for slavery. In his opinion, civil rights laws and affirmative action have provided some practical remedies for racial discrimination, but laws in themselves could not address the lingering scars and emotional barriers between whites and blacks. Hall argued that a formal governmental apology to the descendants of African American slaves would be a healthy way to encourage people to work together in bridging the racial divide:

> An apology . . . can foster the goodwill needed to change the future. In giving those wronged the dignity of an honest admission that our nation was mistaken, it can give us all a measure of healing. . . .
>
> "I am sorry" is the first step of any person trying to right a wrong. These words are the foundation for beginning again, part of the price for restoring lost trust, and necessary to move forward constructively. Yet in the case of our nation's greatest moral failing, speaking those words is a step the U.S. has not taken.[54]

Hall's idea is one among several recent recommendations offered by concerned people seeking ways to resolve racial problems in America. During the 1950s and 1960s, African Americans were largely the initiators in civil rights struggles for justice and equal opportunity. However, many of the recent suggestions for racial justice, including Hall's, demand that whites as a group take responsibility for their past and present role in the nation's racial problems.

Is an Apology for Slavery Necessary?

Hall's proposal sparked intense criticism and debate. Many felt that it was absurd to demand that the U.S. government act as a representative for today's whites in apologizing for slavery. As one white critic put it, "I didn't own any slaves. Why should I apologize?"[55]

Representative Tony Hall maintained that a government apology for slavery was "necessary to move forward constructively."

Another commentator insisted, moreover, that it was grossly unfair to ask America to apologize for a phenomenon that existed for centuries in many parts of the world: "Slavery existed all over this planet, among people of every color, religion and nationality. Why then a national apology for a worldwide evil? Is a national apology for murder next?"[56]

Still others argued that an apology, even if sincere, would have little, if any, social impact. "The political, economic, and social injustices which African Americans still endure as a result of centuries of slavery would remain,"[57] claimed the staff of the *Philadelphia Tribune* in a 1997 editorial. During a time of rollbacks in affirmative action policies, many minority advocates maintain that more energy must be spent on concrete solutions such as improved health care for poor people of color and increased funding for low-income schools.

Sobered by the controversy his proposal stirred, Hall reiterated that he did not intend an apology for slavery to substitute for actions that would ensure justice and equal opportunity for African Americans. He stated, furthermore, that he simply wished to help open up more lines of communication between the races: "Talk of [racial] reconciliation is a dialogue of hope, but if it does not begin with an apology, it cannot achieve all that it might. . . . If we cannot agree on this simple step, how can we tackle the thornier issues ahead?"[58]

But Hall was most disturbed by the myriad letters and calls he got from people who were viciously opposed to an apology. Three-quarters of the responses he received included such statements as "I would like to see our nation return to slavery,"[59] and comments that blacks should be grateful for their ancestors' enslavement because without it "they would still be running around over there [in Africa] in loincloths."[60] Although Hall realizes that such responses are not representative of the majority of Americans, he maintains, "If I get all these hate calls over a simple apology, we have a problem."[61]

Differences of Opinion

On occasion, governments do apologize for policies that have harmed certain groups of people. For example, the Canadian government apologized to its Indian population for 150 years of poorly planned education and assistance programs. Canada has promised financial reparations to Canadian Indians who were forced to leave their homes to attend racist schools; it has also promoted social and economic development programs for them. In 1988 the U.S. government granted a formal apology and $1 billion to thousands of Japanese Americans who were forced to live in prison camps during World War II. In 1998 the United States also apologized for conducting secret medical experiments on four hundred black men earlier in the

A Japanese American family in an internment camp during World War II. The U.S. government later apologized to those who were sent to the camps.

twentieth century. Between 1932 and 1972, these men were denied treatment for syphilis to study how the disease progressed. Financial reparations were paid to them and their heirs.

Hall's proposal for a formal apology for slavery, however, failed in Congress. Additionally, a Gallup poll revealed a striking difference of opinion between whites and blacks on the issue of an apology: 67 percent of whites opposed the idea, while 65 percent of blacks favored it. These results are very similar to those recorded in other surveys asking Americans their opinions on affirmative action or increases in civil rights legislation, which whites largely oppose and blacks largely support. As is the case with most racially charged issues, whites and minorities seem to look at the world through different lenses.

Hall believes that many whites opposed his measure because they thought he was advocating financial reparations for the descendants of slaves. Analysts have estimated that such reparations could cost trillions of dollars, an expense that many feel the U.S. economy cannot afford. In actuality, however, the congressman intended the apology to serve only as a gesture of atonement and a point from which to begin a productive public conversation on race. But since previous governmental apologies have involved financial reparations, many assumed an apology for slavery would do the same.

While African Americans have differing opinions about the need for economic compensation, many contend that the opposition to an apology reflects a lack of understanding about slavery's aftermath. "What most people don't realize is that descendants of Africans have spent more time in slavery than being free in this country. And we're [still] dealing with that legacy," contends George E. Curry, editor of *Emerge* magazine. Black congressman John Conyers agrees that whites often fail to look at the past with perspective: "Just as White Americans have benefited from education, life experiences and wealth that was handed down to them by their ancestors, so too have African-Americans been harmed by the institution of slavery."[62]

Should Blacks Be Paid Back for Slavery?

During each year since 1989, John Conyers has submitted a congressional bill entitled the Commission to Study Reparations Proposals for African Americans Act. The bill's intent is to create a

John Conyers proposed a controversial bill regarding reparations to the descendants of slaves.

panel of experts to study the lingering effects of slavery on contemporary U.S. society. The panel would also examine whether a debt is owed to the descendants of slaves, today's African Americans. As of 1999, the bill has never been debated in Congress, but it has drawn considerable interest and controversy.

Supporters maintain that reparations for blacks would be a practical and effective way to redress racial injustices. They argue that the idea of economic compensation is a simple question of fairness: Whites denied blacks income and education during the period of slavery, and slavery's aftermath involved continuing discrimination and economic inequality for blacks; therefore, whites as a group should repay blacks the income they have long been denied. Georgetown University business professor Richard America contends that such compensation is preferable to a statement of apology because "it's not about guilt. It's not about blame. It's not about a lot of emotional stuff. This is a problem of accounting."[63]

Most supporters of reparations would not have the government make payments to individuals. Instead, they argue for benefits such as free college education for several generations of African Americans. Others promote a government reparations fund that would finance school construction, housing, and job training centers for blacks. "The form of reparations that makes sense is an impassioned recommitment to closing the opportunity gap," argues Harvard law professor Christopher Edley Jr. "That's the reparations we are due. Not 40 acres and a mule, but world-class schools for our kids."[64]

Critics, however, point out that government reparations have always been given to survivors—not on behalf of those who have already died. Many also question whether it is fair to ask American taxpayers who never owned slaves to compensate the descendants of slaves. As Illinois congressman Henry Hyde maintains, "I never owned a slave. I never oppressed anybody. I don't know that I should have to pay for someone who did [own slaves] generations before I was born." Pennsylvania senator Rich Santorum agrees, adding, "There have always been bad things that have happened to people. Slavery was awful. But I don't think there is anything to be gained by going backward to try to come up with some way to pay for something that you can't put a monetary price on."[65]

Others argue that it would be too difficult to establish who is a descendant of slaves, making a reparations fund vulnerable to abuse As one commentator put it, "It would literally pay to be black. . . . Everybody and their momma would claim they were black."[66]

Communal Expressions of Regret

Despite strong opposition to a formal apology and reparations for blacks, some individuals and communities have taken it upon themselves to publicly express regret over racism and mistreatment of people of color. The students of Lincoln-Sudbury Regional High School in Massachusetts, for example, created a website featuring "A Letter of Apology for Slavery from the Students of America." The website invites its visitors to gather signatures on behalf of a statement declaring that "we are sorry for what happened to African-Americans at the hands of some of our forebears, or with

*Illinois representative
Henry Hyde opposed
reparations.*

sanction of several of our Founding Fathers. What happened was a crime against humanity."[67]

In explaining their rationale for their website and grassroots effort, the students contend that "we are not so naive as to think that an apology will undo the wrongs that have taken place in the past. We do know, however, that apologies are the first step to healing. What has taken place in our nation's past is a blemish on the country's historical record. We simply mean to point that out and express our regret of that fact."[68]

Popular author and speaker Marianne Williamson agrees that public expressions of regret are a necessary step in healing the hurts of racism. During some of her presentations, Williamson has whites stand and apologize to blacks and Native Americans in the audience for the harm that racism has inflicted on them and their families. One observer of such an event claims that the mood in the room changed in a way I have never before felt in America: There was an almost tangible lightening of tension for both the [minorities] and the whites. It was a mood in which one could actually move on. As one old black woman said, with tears running down her cheeks, "I've been waiting my whole life to hear a white man say that to me."[69]

Beyond Apologies

While apologies may provide emotional relief, experts often contend that apologies have no lasting effect unless followed up with a deeper examination of the realities of racism. Many believe that in order for whites and people of color to better understand why they hold such contrasting opinions about racism, they must share their experiences and thoughts with one another. During such discussions, whites and minorities are given a chance to see each other as individuals with a wide variety of backgrounds and opinions—an experience that can help to undercut racial stereotypes and prejudices.

The idea of encouraging honest communication between whites and minorities as a way to dismantle racism is not new. In the 1980s many corporations, universities, and military bases began using "diversity training" to address racial tensions in workplaces, schools, and neighborhoods. Workplace diversity training programs became especially popular after a 1987 Labor Department report predicted that after the year 2000, 85 percent of new U.S. employees would be women or minorities.

The goal of most diversity training programs is to stop discrimination in the workplace by enhancing workers' understanding of the problems faced by women and people of color. Diversity trainers use a number of tools—including discussions, films, games, and role-playing—to illuminate problems that workers may not be aware of. About two-thirds of major U.S. corporations now run programs designed to stop sexual harassment, ease racial tensions, and reveal discriminatory practices.

Several social organizations, religious groups, and other concerned communities throughout the nation have also taken on their own diversity training projects. Most of them emphasize the need for well-planned, respectful, and sympathetic dialogue between whites and people of color. They believe that racial reconciliation becomes increasingly possible as more individuals become aware of the experiences of people across racial and ethnic lines.

Not Just Polite Talk

Many diversity consultants strongly insist that cross-racial dialogues must do more than encourage polite mixing and friendly conversation. Participants in public forums on race must be able to speak candidly about painful experiences involving racism. Diversity experts maintain that in order for people to talk freely with no fear of reprisal, dialogues must be carefully planned, well structured, and supervised by skilled counselors.

Counselors Andrea Ayvazian and Beverly Daniel Tatum lead public forums and seminars for Communitas Incorporated, a nonprofit organization that provides diversity training and consultation. In their opinion, public dialogues on racism must always begin with

Sergeant Kevin Smith of the New York City Police Department teaches a class in cultural diversity training to police academy students.

an understanding that whites and people of color have vastly different views of the problem. Keeping this in mind, Ayvazian and Tatum open community discussions by asking white participants to listen intently to the people of color. This may seem like an overly obvious request, but Ayvazian and Tatum point out that many whites have little experience listening to minorities without judging them: "Whites need to listen to the stories and the struggles of people of color in their own or surrounding communities. Not judge, debate, defend, solve, or critique, but listen. Through the simple act of listening, the subtle and pervasive nature of [racism] . . . may become evident."[70]

Listening and Believing

Ayvazian and Tatum make one additional request of the whites who participate in cross-racial dialogues: to believe people of color. Again, they point out that listening and believing may sound like an easy thing to do. But many whites, in fact, have absorbed the stereotypical notions that people of color are less intelligent than whites. Because of such stereotypes, whites often fail to take minorities seriously. As Ayvazian and Tatum contend,

> Whites learned to "second guess" people of color, to assume they were smarter, and to dismiss information that they heard from people of color that contradicted their own experience in the world. But, with modeling, guidance, and support, whites can be helped to listen with an open mind. . . . Imagine the difference in our communities if white people started listening intently to people of color and believing that what they were hearing was actually true.[71]

Getting whites to genuinely believe people of color can be an emotionally wrenching process. Community therapist and filmmaker Lee Mun Wah models this process in his 1994 educational film *The Color of Fear*. This award-winning film records a workshop on racism involving eight men—two Asian, two black, two Latino, and two white. It begins with the men of color describing some of their painful experiences with racism. Eventually, one of the white men becomes puzzled about the fact that minorities often feel held back in society because of prejudice and discrimination.

Insisting that he harbors no prejudices, he points out that he does not understand why people of color "can't just be individuals and go out and make a place for themselves." At one point, he tells one of the black men that "you block your own progress by allowing your attitude toward the white man to limit you."[72]

This kind of comment, diversity counselors contend, is representative of the reactions many whites have when confronted with anger over racism. It is a statement that reveals white resistance to believing what people of color say about discrimination. Rather than accepting that the men of color might have really been held back by racism, the white man prefers to blame minorities for blocking their own progress.

Participating as a facilitator in this filmed workshop, Mun Wah asks the resistant white man to explain why he is unable to believe that people of color are facing serious discrimination. He does this by requesting the white man to imagine "What if the world were not as you thought? What if [racism] really were that bad?" After some pondering, the white man arrives at an emotional moment of revelation. With tears in his eyes, he answers "[I] don't want to believe that man can be so cruel to himself or his own kind. I don't want to accept that it is that way."[73] In effect, he claims, he has denied that racism is a problem because it would be too painful for him to acknowledge that he lives with ease in such a harsh world.

By the end of the film, this white man admits to the men of color that "when you tell me your experiences, I tend to minimize them so that I don't have to deal with them."[74] This recognition of his own denial about the reality of racism, the other participants point out, exemplifies a significant step toward genuine racial healing between whites and minorities.

The National Dialogue on Race

In 1997 President Bill Clinton announced the beginning of a year-long national "Initiative on Race." Arguing that the public needed to face "the implications of Americans of so many races living and working together as we approach a new century,"[75] Clinton established a multiracial advisory panel of seven community leaders to assist in the initiative. This panel was to collect information on racial issues, promote a national dialogue on race, and recommend concrete solutions to racial problems.

The countrywide dialogue on race included a series of nationally televised "town meetings" in which participants were encouraged to discuss their experiences with racism and suggest ways to resolve local racial tensions. These meetings were loosely modeled on the ideas espoused by Ayvazian, Tatum, and Mun Wah: that people of color need to have their racial wounds acknowledged, that whites need to take a more active role in redressing racism, and that minorities and whites must work together to increase multiracial tolerance and understanding.

The president's Initiative on Race garnered much support from many individuals and organizations committed to racial reconciliation. But it also received a good dose of criticism from several quarters. Many believe, for instance, that most community dialogues on race amount to nothing more than group-therapy-like "whine" sessions. Such allegedly healing discussions, critics claim, simply

President Bill Clinton launched his "Initiative on Race" to address racial issues.

encourage exaggerated complaints from people of color who are allowed to bash whites for harboring hidden racist feelings. In the opinion of news columnist Charles Krauthammer, the whole idea of a national conversation on race was "nonsense": "We need more civility, not more self-expression. . . . What the President should be preaching is racial decency. Respect. Restraint. Manners. America's problem is not inhibition. It's exhibition." [76]

Others argued, conversely, that the call for a government-mandated dialogue was too timid. Law professor Bill Ong Hing mused that while the government has declared a "war on drugs," it cannot seem to muster up the energy to declare war on racism. "We all agree that racism is wholly and completely unacceptable," says Ong Hing. "Then where is the sense of urgency over this issue? Where is the sense of outrage and indignation? . . .Where is the commitment of millions of dollars to shock the conscience of America on this issue?" [77] Many critics who agree with Ong Hing also contend that the initiative and the dialogue needed to focus more on such pressing issues as economic and educational inequities faced by minorities.

Still others, particularly nonblack minorities, felt left out of the dialogue. Puerto Rican activist Jose Medina maintains that the presidential initiative failed to include fair representation from the Latino, Asian, and Native American communities. "Today and into the 21st century," states Medina, "the issue of racism must not focus solely on the problems of black and white Americans, but also on other growing minority groups that . . . continue to struggle against discrimination and other forms of racism." [78]

Constructive Criticism About Dialogues and Antiracism Workshops

In thinking about ways to improve antiracism dialogues, some white and minority experts have questioned some of the premises of diversity counseling. Too often, these experts contend, whites are not given permission to talk about their own experiences, and dialogues are carried out in a way that leaves whites feeling guilty about racism. In the worst cases, argues white activist Joe Summers, "anti-racism workshops have encouraged a kind of self-hatred, or self-loathing, among whites." [79] Self-loathing and guilt can be emotionally paralyzing,

Columnist William Raspberry asserted that blame and guilt are counterproductive to building racial equality.

leaving whites powerless to make constructive changes or build healthy partnerships with people of color. While whites should be led to understand that they enjoy "invisible privileges" because of discrimination against minorities, they should not end up believing that they are personally responsible for the existence of racism, Summers maintains.

African American columnist William Raspberry agrees with Summers, pointing out that "people who might be moved to help remedy racial inequality are not inclined to do so if it means acknowledging that the inequality is their fault." Raspberry believes that many of today's blacks also make the mistake of seeing whites as villains "when we—and most particularly our children—would be much better off recruiting allies."[80]

Breaching the Racial Divide

Americans continue to disagree about approaches to breaching the racial divide, but many of them are willing to admit that racial prejudice and privilege are serious national problems. Individuals and communities that promote racial reconciliation maintain that there is no one best way to combat racism in the United States. They argue instead that confronting stereotypes, discrimination, and racial disparities will require a concert of strategies. Perhaps the one thing that most concerned parties can agree on is the need to continue opening lines of communication between whites and people of color.

Conclusion

Is There Hope for Race Relations?

SOCIAL OBSERVERS CAN FIND MANY reasons to feel pessimistic about racism and race relations. Many lament, for example, the apparent failure of efforts to integrate American schools. What represented a civil rights victory in 1954—the Supreme Court ruling that racially segregated education violated the Constitution—seems to be an unfulfilled promise today.

The failure of school desegregation, many contend, is glaringly obvious when looking at the lives of black and white students. "Just as our neighborhoods are separated by race, so too are our schools," maintain authors Leonard Steinhorn and Barbara Diggs-Brown. "Millions of black children attend schools with few or no whites. Millions more white children attend schools with few or no blacks. Whites rarely constitute more than 15 percent of the students in our nation's largest urban school districts, and most of the time they attend predominantly white schools in their own corner of the city. In the South, nearly two-thirds of blacks attend majority-black schools."[81]

Even those students who attend racially mixed schools often find that they live segregated lives. Whites and blacks tend to hang out with others of their own race. Tables at lunchtime in school cafeterias are usually all-white or all-black. Whites who spend time with blacks are accused of being "wanna-bes," and blacks who socialize with whites are mocked for "bleaching out."

Students often maintain that they see no real problem with self-segregation, that they simply prefer to be with others with whom they share the most in common. And some analysts contend that

Teenagers usually befriend those with whom they have the most in common, which can lead to a kind of self-segregation.

minority youths actually have a need for self-segregation, believing that it can help them develop a healthy self-concept free of the negative stereotypes held by whites. But others point out that the sharp differences of opinion that whites and minorities have over racial issues result from one race's lack of experience with the other. Many wonder how the problems of racism will ever be resolved if people of different races—particularly young people—continue to avoid one another.

Despite these distressing truths about the often-segregated lives of students today, some people remain hopeful about race relations. Many historians point out that although blacks and whites do not always see eye to eye, the most celebrated leaps in racial progress customarily involve the efforts of members of each race. The anti-slavery movement and the civil rights movement, for instance, resulted from the hard work of both blacks and whites.

As a result of the legal reforms fostered by the civil rights movement, more blacks and other minorities have access to quality education than ever before in history. This education is enabling them to take on careers as lawyers, scientists, physicians, politicians, teachers, writers, and executives. Professionals of color are diversifying the workplace—and many of them are also using their hard-won skills to help reduce racial inequities and fight for social justice.

A growing number of whites, moreover, are joining the struggle to resolve racial problems. One recent example of this includes a 1997 lawsuit filed by seven white police officers on behalf of their African American and female colleagues. The white officers charged that their supervisor made racist and degrading remarks about their coworkers. Although a district court ruled that the men had no right to sue because the insults were not aimed at them, the officers appealed the decision and won.

Educator and author Robin Kelley believes that all Americans should feel encouraged by the fact that whites have fought and continue to fight for racial justice. In his courses on black history, for example, Kelley reminds his students that during the early battles against segregation in public facilities, "some white people . . . went to the back of the bus, and sat and were arrested or ejected because they wouldn't move from the back of the bus." Numerous whites, Kelley points out, recognized that the civil rights movement "was also for their own liberation, their ability to treat all people with humanity." [82]

Black law professor Randall Kennedy maintains that it is essential for Americans to adopt an optimistic attitude about race relations. He insists that such optimism

> does not ignore racism in its numerous guises. Nor does it privatize public matters, shifting blame to individuals for social disasters. Rather, the optimism I envision is one that acknowledges our massive problems but also recognizes that, through intelligent collective action, we can meet and overcome them. . . . We can realistically expect to build on past accomplishments and press further. [83]

The hundreds of multiracial organizations and coalitions that have sprung up since the late 1980s seem to reflect this optimism.

Some experts believe that the greatest steps toward ending discrimination and achieving true equality are the result of the active efforts of people of all races.

The organization Building Just Communities, for example, was established in 1996 in Minneapolis to reverse that city's growing trend of poverty and racial segregation. Another group, the Cleveland Residential Housing and Mortgage Credit Project, is an effort to bring white and minority realtors together to reduce barriers to racially equitable home ownership. The Community Enhancement Program of Flint, Michigan, uses public forums to engage its citizens in dialogues on race. And the Multicultural Youth Project of Chicago, Illinois, promotes multiethnic understanding among the city's immigrant and refugee youth.

Although many Americans have grown disheartened about find-
ing solutions to racial problems, the continuing work of individuals
and organizations that champion racial justice suggests that there is
hope for race relations. As journalist Clarence Page maintains, interracial cooperation "begins with a refusal to allow the few people or
issues that divide us to get in the way of the many concerns we have
in common."[84]

NOTES

Introduction: Defining Racism

1. Quoted in Juan Williams, *Eyes on the Prize: America's Civil Rights Years, 1954–1965.* New York: Penguin, 1988, p. 52.
2. Quoted in Carl Rowan, "Lessons of a Texas Atrocity," *Liberal Opinion Week*, June 22, 1998, p. 2.
3. Rowan, "Lessons of a Texas Atrocity," p. 2.
4. Quoted in Beverly Daniel Tatum, *"Why Are All the Black Kids Sitting Together in the Cafeteria?" and Other Conversations About Race.* New York: BasicBooks, 1997, p. 7.
5. Tatum, *"Why Are All the Black Kids Sitting Together in the Cafeteria?"* p. 7.
6. Jennifer Hurley, ed., *Racism: Current Controversies.* San Diego: Greenhaven, 1998, p. 14.
7. Quoted in Mary Williams, ed., *Minorities: Current Controversies.* San Diego: Greenhaven, 1998, p. 55.
8. Roper Center at University of Connecticut, "Washington Post, Harvard, Kaiser Race Relations Poll," June 12, 1997. http://web.lexis-nexis.com/univers...4aca437ad071d03b503fe0&taggedDocs=.

Chapter 1: How Serious a Problem Is Racism?

9. Quoted in Mark Hosenball, "It Is Not the Act of a Few Bad Apples," *Newsweek*, May 17, 1999, p. 34.
10. *American Renaissance*, "Police Bias? Says Who?" July 1999, p. 5.
11. Clarence Page, "Bridging Gaps Between Blacks and Whites," *Liberal Opinion Week*, November 9, 1998, p. 12.
12. Quoted in Jennifer Lynn Eberhardt and Susan T. Fiske, eds.,

Confronting Racism: The Problem and the Response. Thousand Oaks, CA: Sage, 1998, p. 4.

13. Quoted in Joe R. Feagin and Hernan Vera, *White Racism: The Basics.* New York: Routledge, 1995, p. 137.
14. David K. Shipler, *A Country of Strangers: Blacks and Whites in America.* New York: Knopf, 1997, p. 487.
15. Quoted in Mikal Muharrar, "'Racial Profiling' in News Reporting," *Extra!* September/October 1998, p. 8.
16. Muharrar, "'Racial Profiling' in News Reporting," p. 8.
17. Muharrar, "'Racial Profiling' in News Reporting," p. 8.
18. Linda Chavez, "Hispanics and the American Dream," *Imprimis,* November 1996, p. 4.
19. Quoted in President's Advisory Board on Race, *One America in the Twenty-First Century: Forging a New Future: The President's Initiative on Race, the Advisory Board's Report to the President* (government document). Washington, DC: The Board, 1998, p. 46.
20. Quoted in President's Advisory Board on Race, *One America in the Twenty-First Century,* p. 47.
21. Quoted in Joe R. Feagin and Melvin P. Sikes, *Living with Racism: The Black Middle-Class Experience.* Boston: Beacon, 1994, p. 72.
22. Quoted in Feagin and Vera, *White Racism,* p. 141.
23. Shipler, *A Country of Strangers,* p. 448.
24. Andrea Ayvazian and Beverly Daniel Tatum, "Can We Talk?" *Sojourners,* January/February 1996, p. 19.

Chapter 2: Can America Accept Its Increasing Racial Diversity?

25. Quoted in Frank H. Wu, "Birthright Citizenship Is Equal Citizenship," unpublished paper, 1996.
26. Quoted in Steven A. Holmes, "Census Sees a Profound Ethnic Shift in the U.S.," *New York Times,* March 14, 1996, p. A8.
27. Timothy Tseng and David Yoo, "The Changing Face of America," *Sojourners,* March/April 1998, p. 28.
28. Bill Clinton, commencement speech to the graduates of the University of California at San Diego, June 14, 1997.
29. Pete Wilson, "Securing Our Nation's Borders," a speech delivered at the Los Angeles Townhall, April 25, 1994.

30. Dick Mountjoy, Ronald Prince, and Barbara Kiley, "Argument in Favor of Proposition 187," California Voter Information Pamphlet, 1994.
31. Quoted in Editors of Sojourners, *America's Original Sin: A Study on White Racism.* Washington, DC: Sojourners, 1995, p. 148.
32. Wilson, "Securing Our Nation's Borders."
33. Quoted in Williams, *Minorities*, p. 152.
34. Quoted in Williams, *Minorities*, p. 162.
35. Quoted in Williams, *Minorities*, p. 158.
36. Guillermo Gomez-Pena, "Beyond the Tortilla Curtain," *Utne Reader*, September/October 1995, p. 39.
37. Quoted in Editors of Sojourners, *America's Original Sin,* p. 154.
38. Alvin J. Schmidt, *The Menace of Multiculturalism: Trojan Horse in America.* Westport, CT: Greenwood, 1997, pp. 44–45.

Chapter 3: Does Affirmative Action Counteract Racial Discrimination?

39. *World & I*, "Key Dates in the History of Affirmative Action," June 1998, p. 27.
40. Quoted in *World & I*, "Race *Should* Be Used for Governmental Decision Making: An Interview with Paul Butler," September 1998, p. 310.
41. Tatum, *"Why Are All the Black Kids Sitting Together in the Cafeteria?"* p. 117.
42. Quoted in David Wagner, "At the Crossroads," *World & I*, June 1998, p. 25.
43. Hilary O. Shelton, "Affirmative Action: It's Still Needed," *World & I*, June 1998, p. 30.
44. Roger Clegg, "Affirmative Action: It's Counterproductive," *World & I*, June 1998, p. 35.
45. Leonard Steinhorn and Barbara Diggs-Brown, *By the Color of Our Skin: The Illusion of Integration and the Reality of Race.* New York: Penguin, 1999, pp. 195–96.
46. Steinhorn and Diggs-Brown, *By the Color of Our Skin*, pp. 195–96.
47. Steven Yates, *Civil Wrongs: What Went Wrong with Affirmative Action.* San Francisco: Institute for Contemporary Studies, 1994, p. 2.

48. Julian Bond, "To Eliminate Unfair Advantage," *World & I*, June 1998, p. 36.
49. Shipler, *A Country of Strangers*, pp. 492–93.
50. Ward Connerly, "With Liberty and Justice *for All*," Heritage Lecture Series, no. 560, March 8, 1996.
51. Quoted in *World & I*, "Race *Should* Be Used for Governmental Decision Making," p. 310.
52. Quoted in Hurley, *Racism*, p. 136.
53. Clegg, "Affirmative Action," p. 34.

Chapter 4: How Can Society Curtail Racism?

54. Tony P. Hall, "An Apology Long Overdue," July 9, 1997, www1.nando.net/newsroom/ntn/voices/070997/voice5_2289.html.
55. Quoted in Naomi Wolf, "Who's Sorry Now?" *George*, August 1998, p. 46.
56. Thomas Sowell, "Apologize for What?" www.unitedstrike.com/Slavery/slave.htm.
57. *Philadelphia Tribune*, "Apology, Even if Sincere, Would Now Be Meaningless" (editorial), August 15, 1997. www.phila-tribune.com/81597oe.html.
58. Hall, "An Apology Long Overdue."
59. Quoted in Sonya Ross, "Walter Mears: An Apology for Slavery Could Explode," *News Times*, July 12, 1997. www.newstimes.com/archive97/jul1297/nad.htm.
60. Quoted in Cynthia Tucker, "Racism Still Rages on, Without Apology," *Liberal Opinion Week*, August 18, 1997, p. 4.
61. Quoted in Ross, "An Apology for Slavery Could Explode."
62. Quoted in George E. Curry, "A Better Way to Apologize," *Emerge*, September 1997, p. 8.
63. Quoted in Kevin Merida, "Did Freedom Alone Pay a Nation's Debt? Rep. John Conyers Jr. Has a Question. He's Willing to Wait a Long Time for the Right Answer," *Washington Post*, November 23, 1999, pp. C01+.
64. Quoted in Merida, "Did Freedom Alone Pay a Nation's Debt?" pp. C01+.
65. Quoted in Merida, "Did Freedom Alone Pay a Nation's Debt?" pp. C01+.

66. Quoted in Merida, "Did Freedom Alone Pay a Nation's Debt?" pp. C01+.

67. Lincoln-Sudbury Regional High School, "A Letter of Apology for Slavery from the Students of America." http://members.tripod.com/~slavery_apology/index.html.

68. Lincoln-Sudbury Regional High School, "Why We're Doing This." http://members.tripod.com/~slavery_apology/info.html.

69. Wolf, "Who's Sorry Now?" pp. 46–47.

70. Ayvazian and Tatum, "Can We Talk?" p. 18.

71. Ayvazian and Tatum, "Can We Talk?" pp. 18–19.

72. Quoted in Lee Mun Wah, *The Color of Fear* (film). Oakland, CA: Stir-Fry Productions, 1994.

73. Quoted in Mun Wah, *The Color of Fear*.

74. Quoted in Mun Wah, *The Color of Fear*.

75. Bill Clinton, commencement speech to the graduates of the University of California at San Diego.

76. Quoted in Andrea Lewis, "Talking About Race," *Third Force*, March/April 1998, p. 38.

77. Bill Ong Hing, "Where Is the Declaration of War?" *Poverty and Race*, November/December 1998, p. 3.

78. Quoted in Minorities' Job Bank, "Jose Medina Urges President to Extend Initiative on Race." www.minorities-jb.com/native/news/medina.html.

79. Joe Summers, "Unpacking Anti-Racism," *Witness*, July/August 1998, p. 24.

80. William Raspberry, "The Difference Between Solving Problems and Making Enemies," *Liberal Opinion Week*, January 5, 1998, p. 5.

Conclusion: Is There Hope for Race Relations?

81. Steinhorn and Diggs-Brown, *By the Color of Our Skin*, p. 43.

82. Quoted in Jane Slaughter, "Complicating the Stories: An Interview with Robin Kelley," *Witness*, April 1997, p. 13.

83. Randall Kennedy, "Race: A Case for Optimism," *Responsive Community*, Summer 1996, p. 10.

84. Clarence Page, "Still Partners After All These Years," *Liberal Opinion Week*, May 18, 1997, p. 18.

ORGANIZATIONS TO CONTACT

American Civil Liberties Union (ACLU)
125 Broad St., 18th Fl.
New York, NY 10004
(212) 549-2500
fax: (212) 549-2646
website: www.aclu.org

The ACLU is a national organization that works to defend Americans' civil rights as guaranteed by the U.S. Constitution. The ACLU publishes and distributes policy statements, pamphlets, and the semiannual newsletter *Civil Liberties Alert.*

Amnesty International (AI)
322 Eighth Ave.
New York, NY 10004-2400
(212) 807-8400
(800) AMNESTY (266-3789)
fax: (212) 627-1451
website: www.amnesty-usa.org

Founded in 1961, AI is a grassroots activist organization that aims to free all nonviolent people who have been imprisoned because of their beliefs, ethnic origin, sex, color, or language. The *Amnesty International Report* is published annually, and other reports are available on-line and by mail.

Cato Institute
1000 Massachusetts Ave. NW
Washington, DC 20001-5403

(202) 842-0200
fax: (202) 842-3490
e-mail: cato@cato.org
website: www.cato.org

The Cato Institute believes in limiting the control of government and protecting individual liberties. It researches claims of discrimination and opposes affirmative action. The institute offers numerous publications, including the *Cato Journal*, the bimonthly newsletter *Cato Policy Report*, and the quarterly magazine *Regulation*.

Citizens' Commission on Civil Rights (CCCR)
2000 M St. NW, Suite 400
Washington, DC 20036
(202) 659-5565
fax: (202) 223-5302
e-mail: citizens@cccr.org
website: www.cccr.org

The CCCR monitors the federal government's enforcement of antidiscrimination laws and promotes equal opportunity for all. It publishes reports on affirmative action and desegregation as well as the book *One Nation Indivisible: The Civil Rights Challenge for the 1990s*.

Commission for Racial Justice (CRJ)
700 Prospect Ave.
Cleveland, OH 44115-1110
(216) 736-2100
fax: (216) 736-2171

The CRJ was formed in 1963 by the United Church of Christ in response to racial tensions gripping the nation at that time. Its goal is a peaceful, dignified society where all men and women are equal. The CRJ publishes various documents and books, such as *Racism and the Pursuit of Racial Justice* and *A National Symposium on Race and Housing in the United States: Challenges for the Twenty-First Century*.

Heritage Foundation
214 Massachusetts Ave. NE

Washington, DC 20002-4999
(202) 546-4400
fax: (202) 546-8328
e-mail: info@heritage.org
website: www.heritage.org

The foundation is a public policy research institute that advocates limited government and the free-market system. It believes that the private sector, not government, should be relied upon to ease social problems. The Heritage Foundation publishes the quarterly *Policy Review* as well as numerous monographs, books, and papers.

Hispanic Policy Development Project (HPDP)
1001 Connecticut Ave. NW, Suite 901
Washington, DC 20036
(202) 822-8414
fax: (202) 822-9120

The HPDP encourages the analysis of public policies affecting Hispanics in the United States, particularly the education, training, and employment of Hispanic youth. It publishes a number of books and pamphlets, including *Together Is Better: Building Strong Partnerships Between Schools and Hispanic Parents.*

National Association for the Advancement of Colored People (NAACP)
4805 Mt. Hope Dr.
Baltimore, MD 21215-3297
(410) 358-8900
fax: (410) 486-9257

The NAACP is the oldest and largest civil rights organization in the United States. Its principal objective is to ensure the political, educational, social, and economic equality of minorities. It publishes the magazine *Crisis* ten times a year as well as a variety of newsletters, books, and pamphlets.

National Network for Immigrant and Refugee Rights (NNIRR)
310 Eighth St., Suite 307

Oakland, CA 94607
(510) 465-1984
fax: (510) 465-1885
e-mail: nnir@igc.apc.org
website: www.nnir.org

The network includes community, church, labor, and legal groups committed to the cause of equal rights for all immigrants. These groups work to end discrimination and unfair treatment of illegal immigrants and refugees. It publishes a monthly newsletter, *Network News*.

National Urban League
120 Wall St., 8th Fl.
New York, NY 10005
(212) 558-5300
fax: (212) 344-5332
website: www.nul.org

A community service agency, the National Urban League aims to eliminate institutional racism in the United States. It also provides services for minorities who experience discrimination in employment, housing, welfare, and other areas. It publishes the report *The Price: A Study of the Costs of Racism in America* and the annual *State of Black America*.

Poverty and Race Research Action Council (PRRAC)
3000 Connecticut Ave., Suite 200
Washington, DC 20008
(202) 387-9887
fax: (202) 387-0764
e-mail: info@prrac.org.

PRRAC is a national organization that promotes research and advocacy on the behalf of poor minorities. It publishes the bimonthly *Poverty and Race*.

Prejudice Institute
Stephens Hall Annex, TSU

Towson, MD 21204-7097
(410) 830-2435
fax: (410) 830-2455

The Prejudice Institute is a national research center concerned with
violence and intimidation motivated by prejudice. It publishes
research reports, bibliographies, and the quarterly newsletter *Forum*.

United States Commission on Civil Rights
624 Ninth St. NW, Suite 500
Washington, DC 20425
(202) 376-7533
publications: (202) 376-8128

A fact-finding body, the commission reports directly to Congress
and the president on the effectiveness of equal opportunity laws and
programs. A catalog of its numerous publications can be obtained
from its Publication Management Division.

For Further Reading

Jim Carnes, *Us and Them: A History of Intolerance in America*. New York: Oxford University Press, 1999. For young adults. Each chapter focuses on an individual's experience with prejudice or a specific historical incident involving bigotry.

Ellis Cose, *Color-Blind: Seeing Beyond Race in a Race-Obsessed World*. New York: Harperperennial Library, 1998. Black *Newsweek* columnist Cose draws on his own experiences as well as recent events in South Africa and Brazil in a provocative examination of racism.

Clyde W. Ford, *We* Can *All Get Along: Fifty Steps You Can Take to Help End Racism*. New York: Dell, 1994. Discusses strategies for how individuals, families, and communities can combat racism.

Paul Kivel, *Uprooting Racism: How White People Can Work for Racial Justice*. New York: New Society, 1995. Offers practical suggestions for how white people can intervene when racism occurs at work, in schools, and in neighborhoods.

Laughlin McDonald, *The Rights of Racial Minorities*. New York: Puffin, 1998. Part of the American Civil Liberties Union Handbooks for Young Americans series. Documents the legal battles waged by Americans of color to obtain civil rights and political representation.

Elaine Pascoe, *Racial Prejudice: Why Can't We Overcome*. Danbury, CT: Franklin Watts, 1997. For young adults. Uses a historical examination of racism as a basis from which to discuss

99

stereotypes, prejudice, and discrimination against minority Americans.

Patricia Raybon, *My First White Friend: Confessions on Race, Love, and Forgiveness.* New York: Penguin, 1997. African American journalist Raybon details how she came to the decision to stop hating and start forgiving white people.

WORKS CONSULTED

Books

Jennifer Lynn Eberhardt and Susan T. Fiske, eds., *Confronting Racism: The Problem and the Response*. Thousand Oaks, CA: Sage, 1998. An anthology of essays by social scientists, psychologists, and other experts detailing the nature of prejudice, discrimination, and racial oppression.

Editors of *Sojourners, America's Original Sin: A Study Guide on White Racism*. Washington, DC: Sojourners, 1995. An anthology of articles addressing such issues as racism, discrimination, integration, and social justice.

Joe R. Feagin and Melvin P. Sikes, *Living with Racism: The Black Middle-Class Experience*. Boston: Beacon, 1994. A study based on the testimony of hundreds of black respondents showing how racial discrimination affects African Americans at school, at work, and in public spaces.

Joe R. Feagin and Hernan Vera, *White Racism: The Basics*. New York: Routledge, 1995. This book presents several case studies of racial discrimination committed by middle-class whites against African Americans.

Jennifer Hurley, ed., *Racism: Current Controversies*. San Diego: Greenhaven, 1998. An anthology of articles that includes various viewpoints on racism, discrimination, affirmative action, and suggestions for improving race relations.

Alvin J. Schmidt, *The Menace of Multiculturalism: Trojan Horse in America*. Westport, CT: Greenwood, 1997. This author condemns multiculturalism as a misguided ideology that could

101

eventually lead to serious and potentially violent conflicts between different racial and ethnic groups.

David K. Shipler, *A Country of Strangers: Blacks and Whites in America*. New York: Knopf, 1997. *New York Times* journalist Shipler recounts his five-year journey across the United States listening and talking to black and white Americans about integration, segregation, stereotypes, and potential remedies for racism.

Leonard Steinhorn and Barbara Diggs-Brown, *By the Color of Our Skin: The Illusion of Integration and the Reality of Race*. New York: Penguin, 1999. An analytical and provocative discussion of American race relations that examines why blacks and whites view racial problems differently.

Beverly Daniel Tatum, *"Why Are All the Black Kids Sitting Together in the Cafeteria?" and Other Conversations About Race*. New York: BasicBooks, 1997. Tatum, a renowned expert on the psychology of racism, explains why young people of color have a need to affirm a racial identity that is free of negative stereotypes. She also discusses how whites can actively promote racial justice.

Juan Williams, *Eyes on the Prize: America's Civil Rights Years, 1954–1965*. New York: Penguin, 1988. A companion text to the PBS television series, this book is a detailed narrative account of the first ten years of the U.S. civil rights movement.

Mary Williams, ed., *Minorities: Current Controversies*. San Diego: Greenhaven, 1998. An anthology of essays presenting diverse viewpoints on race relations, bilingual education, policies affecting minorities, and America's changing racial demographics.

Steven Yates, *Civil Wrongs: What Went Wrong with Affirmative Action*. San Francisco: Institute for Contemporary Studies, 1994. This author argues that affirmative action policies create de facto racial quotas that discriminate against white males.

Government Documents

Dick Mountjoy, Ronald Prince, and Barbara Kiley, "Argument in Favor of Proposition 187," California Voter Information Pamphlet, 1994.

President's Advisory Board on Race, *One America in the Twenty-First Century: Forging a New Future: The President's Initiative on Race, the Advisory Board's Report to the President.* Washington, DC: The Board, 1998.

Periodicals

American Renaissance, "Police Bias? Says Who?" July 1999.

Andrea Ayvazian and Beverly Daniel Tatum, "Can We Talk?" *Sojourners*, January/February 1996.

Julian Bond, "To Eliminate Unfair Advantage," *World & I*, June 1998.

Linda Chavez, "Hispanics and the American Dream," *Imprimis*, November 1996.

Roger Clegg, "Affirmative Action: It's Counterproductive," *World & I*, June 1998.

George E. Curry, "A Better Way to Apologize," *Emerge*, September 1997.

Guillermo Gomez-Pena, "Beyond the Tortilla Curtain," *Utne Reader*, September/October 1995.

Steven A. Holmes, "Census Sees a Profound Ethnic Shift in the U.S.," *New York Times*, March 14, 1996.

Mark Hosenball, "It Is Not the Act of a Few Bad Apples," *Newsweek*, May 17, 1999.

Randall Kennedy, "Race: A Case for Optimism," *Responsive Community*, Summer 1996.

Andrea Lewis, "Talking About Race," *Third Force*, March/April 1998.

Kevin Merida, "Did Freedom Alone Pay a Nation's Debt? Rep. John Conyers Jr. Has a Question. He's Willing to Wait a Long Time for the Right Answer," *Washington Post*, November 23, 1999.

Mikal Muharrar, "'Racial Profiling' in News Reporting," *Extra!* September/October 1998.

Bill Ong Hing, "Where Is the Declaration of War?" *Poverty and Race*, November/December 1998.

Clarence Page, "Bridging Gaps Between Blacks and Whites," *Liberal Opinion Week*, November 9, 1998.

———, "Still Partners After All These Years," *Liberal Opinion Week*, May 18, 1997.

William Raspberry, "The Difference Between Solving Problems and Making Enemies," *Liberal Opinion Week*, January 5, 1998.

Carl Rowan, "Lessons of a Texas Atrocity," *Liberal Opinion Week*, June 22, 1998.

Hilary O. Shelton, "Affirmative Action: It's Still Needed," *World & I*, June 1998.

Jane Slaughter, "Complicating the Stories: An Interview with Robin Kelley," *Witness*, April 1997.

Joe Summers, "Unpacking Anti-Racism," *Witness*, July/August 1998.

Timothy Tseng and David Yoo, "The Changing Face of America," *Sojourners*, March/April 1998.

Cynthia Tucker, "Racism Still Rages on, Without Apology," *Liberal Opinion Week*, August 18, 1997.

David Wagner, "At the Crossroads," *World & I*, June 1998.

Naomi Wolf, "Who's Sorry Now?" *George*, August 1998.

World & I, "Key Dates in the History of Affirmative Action," June 1998.

———, "Race *Should* Be Used for Governmental Decision Making: An Interview with Paul Butler," September 1998.

Frank H. Wu, "Birthright Citizenship Is Equal Citizenship," unpublished paper, 1996.

Films

Lee Mun Wah, *The Color of Fear*. Oakland, CA: Stir-Fry Productions, 1994.

Speeches

Bill Clinton, commencement speech to the graduates of the University of California at San Diego, June 14, 1997.

Ward Connerly, "With Liberty and Justice *for All*," Heritage Lecture Series, no. 560, March 8, 1996.

Pete Wilson, "Securing Our Nation's Borders," a speech delivered at the Los Angeles Townhall, April 25, 1994.

Websites

Tony P. Hall, "An Apology Long Overdue," July 9, 1997. www1. nando.net/newsroom/ntn/voices/070997/voices5_2289.html.

Lincoln-Sudbury Regional High School, "A Letter of Apology for Slavery from the Students of America." http://members.tripod. com/~slavery_apology/index.html.

————, "Why We're Doing This." http://members.tripod.com/~ slavery_apology/info.html.

Minorities' Job Bank, "Jose Medina Urges President to Extend Initiative on Race." www.minorities-jb.com/native/news/medina.html.

Philadelphia Tribune, "Apology, Even if Sincere, Would Now Be Meaningless" (editorial), August 15, 1997. www.phila-tribune. com/81597oe.html.

Roper Center at University of Connecticut, "Washington Post, Harvard, Kaiser Race Relations Poll," June 12, 1997. http://web. lexis-nexis.com/univers...4aca437ad071d03b503fe0taggedDocs=.

Sonya Ross, "Walter Mears: An Apology for Slavery Could Explode," *News Times*, July 12, 1997. www.newstimes.com/ archive97/jul1297/nad.htm.

Thomas Sowell, "Apologize for What?" www.unitedstrike.com/ Slavery/slave.htm.

INDEX

Fair Employment Council and
  Urban Institute, 57
Federal Glass Ceiling Commission,
  57
Flint, Michigan, 87

Gallegos, Aaron, 44
Gallup polls, 15, 30, 72
Gilens, Martin, 26
goal-oriented policies, 54, 57–58,
  60
Golden Gate Bridge, 53
Gomez-Pena, Guillermo, 46–47

Hall, Tony P., 68–70, 72
health care, 46
health officials, 57
heroin, 20
hiring practices, 53
Hispanics. *See* Latinos
Hopwood v. Texas, 63, 75
House of Representatives, 68
housing, 61
Hyde, Henry, 74–75

IHOP. *See* International House of
  Pancakes
immigrants, 38–46, 87
inclusive education. *See* culturally
  inclusive education
incomes, of blacks, 30
Indians, 44, 49, 70–71, 81
"Initiative on Race," 79–80
inoculation, 48
International House of Pancakes
  (IHOP), 13
internment camps, 16, 71

Jackson, Jesse, 53
Japanese Americans, 16, 71
Jasper, Texas, 9–12

jobs, 14, 29, 41–42, 44, 54, 57, 61
Johnson, Lyndon, 63
Justice Department, 19

Kelley, Robin, 86
Kennedy, John, 52
Kennedy, Randall, 86
King, Rodney, 22
Krauthammer, Charles, 81

Latinos
  enrollment of, in college, 63, 66
  fair representation of, 81
  as illegal immigrants, 41, 44
  incomes of, 30
  opportunities given to, 14
  police treatment of, 13, 18
  portrayal of, by media, 28
  questioning of, by customs, 36
  whites living among, 45
law enforcement. *See* police
law schools, 53, 63
"Letter of Apology for Slavery
  from the Students of America,
  A," 74
Lewis, Meriwether, 48
Lincoln-Sudbury Regional High
  School, 74
Los Angeles, 22, 27, 42
Louima, Abner, 22–23

managers, 57
Maryland, 19
media, 26–28
medical schools, 55
Medina, Jose, 81
Meredith, James, 25
merit, 63, 65
Mexico, 41
middle class, 30
Minneapolis, 87

PICTURE CREDITS

ABOUT THE AUTHOR

Mary E. Williams earned a master's in fine arts degree from San Diego State University, where she studied comparative literature, poetry, and creative writing. Williams has an enduring interest in race relations, world religions, and social justice. Currently she edits educational texts for Greenhaven Press in San Diego, California, and she is writing a novel. She lives in San Marcos, California, with her husband, Kirk Takvorian, and a pet snake, Raoul.